Instructor's Manual
Interactions 2
Reading

4th Edition

Prepared by
Janet Podnecky

McGraw-Hill
Contemporary

McGraw-Hill/Contemporary
A Division of The McGraw-Hill Companies

Interactions 2 Reading Instructor's Manual, 4th Edition

Published by McGraw-Hill/Contemporary, a business unit of The McGraw-Hill Companies, Inc., 1221 Avenue of the Americas, New York, NY 10020. Copyright © 2002, 1996, 1990, 1985 by The McGraw-Hill Companies, Inc. All rights reserved. No part of this publication may be reproduced or distributed in any form or by any means, or stored in a database or retrieval system, without the prior written consent of The McGraw-Hill Companies, Inc., including, but not limited to, in any network or other electronic storage or transmission, or broadcast for distance learning.

 This book is printed on recycled, acid-free paper containing 10% postconsumer waste.

2 3 4 5 6 7 8 9 0 PBT/PBT 0 9 8 7 6 5 4 3 2

ISBN 0-07-248143-9

Editorial director: *Tina B. Carver*

Series editor: *Annie Sullivan*

Development editors: *Louis Carrillo, Annie Sullivan*

Director of marketing: *Thomas P. Dare*

Production and composition: *A Good Thing, Inc.*

Printer: *Phoenix Color*

www.mhcontemporary.com/interactionsmosaic

TABLE OF CONTENTS

Introduction

Interactions 2 Reading encourages students to become actively involved in their own reading development. Students' thoughts and input are crucial in the reading process. They need to form ideas before reading a selection, pick out important ideas as they read, and finally, consider and discuss critically the main idea—the writer's message. The students are interacting with the reading selections, with the writers' ideas, and with others in the class.

The goal of **Interactions 2 Reading** is for students to become independent readers through instruction in the various reading skills and through intensive and extensive readings. There are pre- and post-reading exercises to develop reading skills and vocabulary. The exercises carefully introduce and model the key skills. Expansion and extension ideas provide additional challenging work to meet the individual needs of more advanced learners.

The reading level is challenging. The selections represent the different learning fields in order to prepare students to use academic textbooks. Students practice identifying main ideas, classifying and organizing information, and preparing summaries—skills needed for academic study and research. Although technical vocabulary may be pre-taught, students are encouraged to use context clues to infer meanings of new vocabulary. Sentence structures include complex and compound sentences that are common in academic texts. Finally, the reading passages express various cultural viewpoints and issues for analysis and class discussion.

General Teaching Suggestions

Teacher's Role

The reading teacher has a multi-faceted role. At times, the teacher needs to give instruction especially about language issues and provide cultural and background information that is important to the topic. Other times, the teacher is a participant listening to and sharing opinions and taking part in class and group discussions. The teacher is also a facilitator, creating a classroom environment that promotes learning and communication. Finally, the teacher provides encouragement and feedback, challenging students to continue developing their reading skills.

Teaching Practices

As your role as teacher changes in the classroom, you will want to adjust the practices you use. With whole class activities, such as large group discussions and sharing of ideas, initial presentations, and comprehension activities, you need to keep students' attention.

- Use volunteers as models and then call on others in the class.
- List important information and words on the board.
- Maintain a lively pace in the class.
- Try to give everyone a chance to participate.

When checking comprehension of reading selections, begin with *yes/no* questions and *or* questions, allowing the beginning level students to answer. Then ask information questions (*wh-* questions: *who, what, when, where, why*). Later, ask questions to the more advanced students that require more critical and creative thinking. These would be questions that involve analyzing, making inferences, and making comparisons. For example: *What would you suggest ...? How do you ...? Why would someone ...?* As you go through the reading selections, you may want to stop after each paragraph to check understanding and to point out and discuss key vocabulary words.

As you review the responses to the student book exercises, ask volunteers to explain their answers and to justify their responses. If appropriate, have the class look back at the readings to verify information and details. In exercises where more than one answer is possible, invite several students to share their responses and ideas.

Groupwork

Small groups allow students more of a chance to participate in discussion activities. It is often easier to speak in a small group than in front of the whole class, so the small group situation is more secure for those who are less proficient in their speaking skills. In addition, it allows time for students to help each other with vocabulary. Students can think and practice saying something in a small group before addressing a larger audience. Groupwork promotes discussion and sharing of ideas and cultural understanding. Students can learn from each other. Groupwork also allows you to address individual needs of students.

When students are working in groups, be sure that:

- students understand the directions of the activity
- everyone in the group is involved or has a role
- students show respect for each other
- there is a time limit for the activity
- groups have a chance to share what they discussed or prepared

Divide the class into groups of 4 – 6 for discussions and group writing activities. Prepare for groupwork. Have the following roles clearly defined for each member of the group:

- *reader,* or *facilitator,* who reads instructions, guides the group, is the leader
- *recorder,* who takes notes on discussions and answers for the activity
- *checker,* who makes sure everyone in the group understands points and watches the time, etc.
- *reporter,* who will share the group's information with the rest of the class

As groups are working, go around the room listening. You may need to assist with vocabulary or give other guidance. Your job is to facilitate the group activity, not to lead it. Make a note of types of problems that arise and address them later.

Vocabulary

Before each of the reading selections, students discuss what they already know about a topic area. Basic vocabulary is reviewed or presented in illustrations and in pre-reading questions. Make a list of words for students to refer to as they work through the chapter. Key vocabulary is listed before each of the readings. It is not necessary for students to study all of these words before doing the reading exercises, but it is helpful for them to check off the words they know

and circle words that are new to them. You may want to have volunteers suggest meanings of words they know. Remind students to look for these key vocabulary words in the reading selections. Often there are context clues, restatements or definitions of the words within the selection. Encourage students to make general guesses about the meanings of the new words based on the context clues. Later, they may want to check a dictionary for the precise meanings. After completing the reading activities, have students look back at the vocabulary lists and check again their understanding of the new words. It is a good way for students to check their understanding and to check their own progress.

Multi-level Classes

Students have different needs and learning styles, so there will usually be a range of levels within a class. By varying the types of activities, you can address the needs of all students. Use whole class activities for presenting and modeling activities. Allow students to work individually, in pairs, or small groups to practice and prepare responses. During this time, give individual attention as needed. Have students work together in cooperative groups, not competitive groups. In this way, all students will participate, contribute, help, and learn from each other rather than competing against each other. If some students finish classwork activities before others in the class, encourage them to work on the expansion and extension suggestions found at the end of many of the student book exercises. You may want to provide additional reading materials for these advanced learners to browse through if they finish earlier than others. If possible, allow students to explore the Internet for related readings and information to share with the class related to the chapter topics.

You may want to ask students to evaluate their own progress halfway through the course. Ask them to write down if they feel they are making progress and what they feel they have learned so far in the course. Also ask them to write down what they hope to achieve in the second half of the course and how you can best help them achieve their goals. As you read through their self-evaluations, make notes about common goals they have to incorporate into the course. Give students feedback on their progress, too.

Using the Video

The video component provides additional activities related to the chapter topics. Each segment presents some culturally significant concept, fact, or issue. You may choose to use the video at the end of the chapter, as a culminating activity that reinforces listening, speaking, reading, and writing skills. The video section may be used at the beginning of a chapter to present the basic content area and initiate discussion of the basic content. Alternatively, you might find it more appropriate to use the video section to break up the heavy reading content and reading skills exercises in the chapter.

For each video segment there are several activities. The first exercise prepares students for watching the video. Students list vocabulary or share information that they know about the topic. They can make predictions about what they will see based on the title and the activity questions. The next two activities guide students as they watch the video at least two times. Students should read the questions before watching so they will know what information they need to find. The video segments are relatively short, so students are encouraged to watch the videos several times. The final video exercise invites students to check for other information related to the video segment in newspapers, magazines, and on the Internet. It leads students to read for information and to apply their reading skills to things outside of the classroom.

Administering the Reading Placement Test

The Reading Placement test helps teachers and administrators place students into the Reading strand of the **Interactions Mosaic** series. All of the placement tests have been carefully designed to assess a student's language proficiency as it correlates to the different levels of the **Interactions Mosaic** series.

The Reading test has been created to assess both vocabulary development skills and reading comprehension skills. The first three parts of the test assess the skills students use to determine word meaning. Part 1 focuses on determining meaning and usage from context. Part 2 narrows in on idiomatic expressions. Part 3 determines whether students can scan for members of word families. The final part of the test, Part 4, assesses reading comprehension and consists of four different reading selections. The selections vary in length and complexity. Students must answer both literal and inferential questions.

The tests follow multiple choice and true/false formats for easy administration and scoring. Use the following charts to place your students in the correct level of text. To maintain test validity, be sure to collect all copies of the test and store the test in a secure location.

Placement Chart for the Reading Test

Number of Items Correct	Place in
0–10	Needs a more basic text.
11–17	Interactions Access
18–24	Interactions 1
25–34	Interactions 2
36–43	Mosaic 1
43–48	Mosaic 2

Using the Chapter Quizzes

The **Interactions 2 Reading** chapter quizzes allow teachers to assess whether the students have mastered the vocabulary and basic comprehension of the reading passages in the chapters. They also assess how well students can use the real-life reading skills or recognize word categories. In addition, they help assess how well students can use the language to communicate in writing their own ideas and thoughts about the chapter topics.

The **Interactions 2 Reading** chapter quizzes do not test students' reading comprehension or summarizing skills. The teacher should be assessing and evaluating students' reading skills progress as they do the exercises in the chapters.

The chapter quizzes also bring closure to chapters and give students a feeling of achievement and progress as they go through the textbook and course.

Description

There are twelve quizzes, one for each chapter in the reading text. Each quiz contains five sections:

- vocabulary
- comprehension
- grammar/structure
- real-life reading skills and categorization
- self-expression

The first section checks students' understanding of key vocabulary about the chapter topics. The vocabulary items are selected from the first two reading selections of the chapter. Students match the words with their meanings or synonyms.

The comprehension section checks general understanding of the key ideas of the first two reading selections of the chapter. The ideas are about the main ideas rather than specific details from the readings. Students decide if statements are true or false.

A major grammar or language structure for each chapter is highlighted in the third section of the quizzes. Students choose the correct form to complete sentences. Some structures tested include: simple present tense forms, prepositions, simple present vs. present progressive verb forms, pronouns, and related words (nouns, verbs, and adjectives). Although there are no exercises in the student book on these specific grammar points, students need to use them throughout the chapter exercises.

The fourth section of the quizzes focuses on the real-life reading activities of the chapters or other reading skills practiced in the chapters, such as categorization, facts and opinions, and sequencing. Students need to be able to recognize and use the words and expressions that are in reading materials around them daily and they need to apply other higher level reading skills.

The last section allows students to write their own personal views and responses to questions related to the chapter topics. The questions give students a chance to reflect on their own experiences and feelings about the chapter topic. Answers will vary from student to student.

Administration

The quizzes can be duplicated and given to students individually or for full-class administration.

Scoring and Grading

Each section of the quiz is worth a specific number of points. The total possible score is 25 points.

Education and Student Life

Goals

- **Read about and discuss educational systems in different countries**
- **Use context clues: parentheses, dashes, commas, logic**
- **Understand main idea**
- **Understand reading structure**
- **Skim for main ideas**
- **Identify topic and topic sentence**
- **Understand pronoun reference**
- **Recognize literal, opinion, and application questions**
- **Scan for information**

Part 1 Education: A Reflection of Society

Before You Read

1 Discussing Pictures. Page 2.

This activity allows students to talk about some pictures related to the chapter topic. As students discuss the pictures and questions, they will share and use basic vocabulary and personal experiences about key concepts of this chapter—education and cultural values. You may want to have students look at the pictures and think about the questions as a homework assignment before doing the group discussion activity.

Arrange students in groups of four or five. Give the groups about 10-15 minutes to discuss the questions. Circulate among the groups, listening, and giving assistance as need. When all groups are finished, ask students to identify the people

and places. Have students tell what the people are doing in each of the pictures. Then read the questions aloud and call on volunteers to answer. Point out key vocabulary: *education, cultural values, primary school, high school, university.* As students suggest answers, record students' responses and ideas on an overhead project or on a large piece of paper. You may want to review these responses later after students have read the selection.

Sample Answers:

1. The first picture is in a primary/elementary school in Africa. The teacher is presenting a lesson on the blackboard. The students are listening and raising their hands to answer the teacher's questions. The second picture is a group of women from Kenya. They are dressed in some traditional clothing. The third picture is a student in a university in England. He is standing in from of an old wooden door or wall. He's holding a newspaper. In the fourth picture, some high school students are working with calculators in a high school. They are all wearing uniforms and doing the same schoolwork. In the U.S. high school, the students are not sitting in a traditional classroom setting. They are a varied group and they are working on a learning project with the teacher.

2. In all of these countries, primary students learn the same subjects: reading, writing, and arithmetic. In high schools, the students begin to work individually on their schoolwork. At the university level, students work more independently as they continue their education. Cultural traditions are taught and practiced in family groups and/or tribes.

3. In Kenya, the education seems more basic skills (reading, writing, and arithmetic) with traditional classrooms. In Japan, the education involves more advanced content with more modern

technology (calculators, computers, etc.). In England, the education may be more classical in content (the humanities: literature, history, philosophy, etc.). In the United States, the teaching style is more informal without traditional paper and pencil work.

4. The cultural values of Kenya seem to be linked to the ethnic tribes and a rural/agricultural life style. In Japan, technology is important. Uniformity and preciseness are values, too. In England, knowledge of the classics seems to be important. In the United States, cooperation and helping each other seems important. Learning by doing something seems more important than learning from books.

2 Vocabulary Preview. Page 3.

Read the words aloud and have students check the ones they don't know. Have students check their understanding of the checked words after they complete the reading selection.

3 Getting Meaning From Context. Page 3.

As you read aloud the explanations, call attention to each of the examples. Ask students look for parentheses, dashes, and commas in the items in Exercise 3. Then read the instructions together. You may want to do the first item together as an example. Read aloud the statement and ask volunteers to suggest what the meaning of "agriculture" is. Remind them to use the information in parentheses to form their definition. Have students complete the exercise individually. If students finish early, have them compare answers with others in the class. As a group, go over the answers. Encourage students to explain how they developed their definitions.

Answers:
1. growing useful products
2. surprise; percentages or other information using numbers; elementary school
3. fee or cost of a school; pay or have enough money for something
4. farming areas or areas not near big cities or towns

5. connection to real life
6. allowing equal opportunities
7. self-control
8. whole or all of; social position or level
9. related to jobs and particular skills for jobs (job training)
10. decides

Read

4 Education: A Reflection of Society. Page 5. [on tape/CD]

Read aloud the instructions and question. Be sure students understand the meaning of "a culture" and "educational system." You may want to have students skim the reading selection, noting the sub-headings to find out which cultures will be discussed in the reading selection. Then, play the tape or CD as students follow along in their books. You may want to stop the recording after every paragraph to check understanding and to point out vocabulary words. Listen a second time as students read along.

After You Read

5 Understanding the Main Idea. Page 6.

Explain "main idea." Read the instructions and have students complete the exercise. Then discuss the answers with the whole class.

Answers: 1. T 2. F 3. T 4. F

Ask students to point out the information that is not true in the false statements. Students can look back in the reading selection for the correct information. Have volunteers restate the false statements to make them true.

6 Understanding Reading Structure. Page 7.

Read together the instructions. Have students look back at the reading selection on pages 5-6 and find the letters for each of the paragraphs before they complete the exercise. Go over the answers with the class.

Answers: 1. f 2. c 3. e 4. b 5. d
6. a

7 Recognizing the Main Idea. Page 7.

Read the instructions together, clarifying as needed. Remind students to check back in the reading's introduction and conclusion for the main ideas. After students have circled their answer, go over the answer with the group. Encourage students to explain their choice.

Answer: 3

8 Page 7.

Go over the instructions together. Ask a volunteer to read the question aloud on page 5. Then have students work in pairs or individually to prepare an answer. Have volunteers read aloud their answers. Make notes on the board as the answers are given. Discuss any variation in content of the answers.

Sample Answer:
By studying an educational system, we can learn about the economy, the social structure, the values, and problems of a particular culture.

Cross-Cultural Note

Read aloud the cultural note on education in North America and Asia. If students have had experiences with or know any additional information about North American and Asian schools, invite them to share with the class. Which points in the note do they feel are the most important or interesting? Would they add anything else to the notes? Which type of a school system do they prefer?

Discussing the Reading

9 Small Group Discussion. Page 8.

This activity allows students to use the vocabulary from the reading to talk about their own experiences related to the content. Arrange students in groups of four.

Assign each person in the group a role:

1. reading the questions to the group; 2. restating answers; 3. recording information; 4. reporting the answers to the whole class. Model the activity and the four roles.

Give the groups about 15-20 minutes to discuss the questions. Circulate among the groups, listening, and giving assistance as need. When all groups are finished, ask the reporters from each group to share the most interesting information form their groups.

Answers will vary.

Part 2 Campus Life in the United States Today

Before You Read

1 Skimming for Main Ideas. Page 8.

Read the directions aloud and go over the example together. Clarify how the topic and topic sentence were selected. Remind students that the topic is usually who or what the paragraph is about and the topic sentence is a sentence that gives the general or main idea of the paragraph.

Read

2 Reading for Topics and Topic Sentences. Page 9. [on tape/cd]

Read the instructions together and go over the example carefully. Depending on the level of the students, you may want to read the paragraphs aloud or play the tape or CD as students follow along in their books. Alternatively, have students work individually reading the paragraphs and identifying the topics and topic sentences. Before going over the answers, you may want to play the recording again, pausing to ask comprehension questions and pointing out key vocabulary. Then, ask volunteers to read the topic and topic sentence for each paragraph. Encourage student explain their choices.

Answers:

A. Topic: College Students and College Life
   Topic sentence: These days the nontraditional students are the majority; they are different from traditional undergraduates in several ways.

B. Topic: Sensing style of learning
   Topic sentence: They prefer a practice-to-theory method of learning—experience first and ideas after that.

C. Topic: Intuitive learning style
   Topic sentence: They prefer a theory-to-practice method of learning and enjoy independent, creative thinking.

D. Topic: Drawback of the sensing style
   Topic sentence: Students in the sensing group are at a disadvantage because their way of thinking doesn't match their teachers'.

E. Topic: Goals of students
   Topic sentence: Today, students seem to be a combination of the two: they want to make good money when they graduate, but they're also interested in helping society.

F. Topic: Technology on campus
   Topic sentence: On all college campuses, student life is very different from what it used to be, due to technology—specifically, the Internet.

After You Read

3 Understanding Pronoun Reference. Page 12.

Read the instructions and call attention to the example. Have students complete the exercise, referring to the reading selection to find the nouns (or nouns phrases) to which the pronouns refer. Go over the answers with the class.

Answers:
1. undergraduate students
2. non-traditional students
3. non-traditional students
4. students (in the sensing group)
5. students (in the 1960s and 1970s)
6. professors

Discussing the Reading

4 Small Group Discussion. Page 12.

Arrange students in groups of four to discuss their answers to the questions. Give the groups about 15-20 minutes to discuss the questions. Circulate among the groups, listening, and giving assistance as needed. When all groups are finished, invite students to share the most interesting information from their groups.

Talk It Over

This activity gives students a chance to express their own opinions and feelings. Read together the instructions about politically correct words and phrases. Model expressing opinions. For example: *I think ____ is not a good word/phrase. It sounds very negative/cruel/sad/neutral/silly/strange/odd. ____ is better because _____.* Ask a volunteer to give his or her thoughts on the words.

Arrange students in groups of four or five to talk about their own thoughts on the politically correct words and phrases. Allow 15-20 minutes for discussion. Allow time for groups to report their ideas. Which words seemed good to your group? Which words seemed strange? As a whole group, summarize the results of the discussions.

Part 3 Building Vocabulary and Study Skills

1 Recognizing Word Meanings. Page 13.
Ask students to complete the exercise on their own. Then discuss the answers with the whole class. Encourage students to use the words in sentences related to the chapter subject: education. In pairs, have students practice the vocabulary. One student reads the word and the partner responds with the definition or synonym. Then have one student say a definition and the other student give the vocabulary word.

Answers: 1. g 2. h 3. i 4. a 5. b
6. d 7. e 8. c 9. j 10. f

2 Words in Context. Page 14.
Read the instructions. You may want to do the first item together as an example. Then, have students work individually on the exercise. Go over the answers and have students suggest other sentences for the vocabulary words.

Answers: 1. primary 2. due to
3. relevance 4. demonstrate 5. vocational
6. value 7. major 8. determine 9. access
10. statistic

Focus on Testing

Answering Questions
In each chapter, there is a section to help students develop test-taking skills. This section encourages students to notice types of questions and gives students tips on how to answer them. Point out that the information and tips will be applicable for tests in other academic areas, too.

Read the instructions together. Explain and give examples of literal, opinion, and application questions. Point out common expressions and question words associated with the various types of questions.

You may want to have students read the questions themselves or you may want to read them aloud. Students should mark the type of question for each item. Then arrange students in small groups to discuss their answers. Go over the answers with the whole class.

As an extension activity, have students prepare two examples for each of the question types to share with the class. Students can use actual questions they have had to answer in other classes or create their own questions based on the reading selections for the chapter. Have a volunteer read the group's questions aloud one at a time for others in the class to identify the types of question.

Answers: 1. op 2. lit 3. lit 4. app
5. lit 6. op 7. app 8. op

Part 4 Reading in the Real World

This part of the chapter provides practice with real reading samples from other academic areas. Students have pre- and post-reading exercises to help with vocabulary development, comprehension, and practical reading skills.

1 Scanning for Information. Page 16.
Read the instructions and questions aloud. Have students make predications about what the reading selection is about. Ask students to read the selection reminding them to look for the information that answers the questions. When students are finished, have them answer the questions. You may want to have students in pairs. Then ask volunteers to give their answers. Discuss any differences students have in their answers. Encourage students to point out the lines from the reading selection where they found the answers.

Sample Answers:
1. The main idea is that there is a standard world curriculum. Children in elementary schools around the world are taught similar subjects.

2. Four countries were part of the study: Israel, Japan, South Korea, and the United States.

3. The group found more similarities than differences in elementary education in these four countries.

4. The same basic subjects were taught: reading, writing, grammar, mathematics, natural sciences, social studies, and foreign language.

5. In the developed countries, there was more stress on arts and physical education. In the developing countries, there was more emphasis on vocational subjects such as agriculture and household work.

2 Getting Meaning from Context. Page 17.

After you read the instructions aloud, have students complete the exercise. Together, go over the answers.

Answers: 2. essentially 3. utilizing
4. data 5. curriculum 6. core
7. outweighed

3 Expanding Vocabulary. Page 18.

Go over the instructions and example clarifying as needed. Remind students to use what they know from the example to create similar words in the exercise without a dictionary. Go over the answers with the entire class.

Answers: 1. nationwide 2. countrywide
3. statewide 4. citywide 5. schoolwide
6. campuswide

Beyond the Text

In each chapter, there is a section about real-life reading materials related to the chapter topic. This section encourages students to look at and use reading materials that are readily available around them. You may want to have students do this as a homework assignment.

Read the instructions aloud. Have students suggest places where they might find or access

the items or information. Allow time in the next class for students to share the samples that they found and talk about vocabulary that they learned from the reading materials.

Video Activities: An Online English Class

Before You Watch

Read the questions aloud and ask students to discuss their answers in small groups. Have students report to the class their answers.

Answers will vary.

Watch [on video]

Ask students to read the list of activities. Then play the video and have them check off the things that students do in the online class. Review the answers together.

Answers: 1. √ 2. — 3. √ 4. √ 5.—
6. √ 7. √

Watch Again [on video]

Point out the chart and explain that students need to watch carefully to find the advantages and disadvantages of the online class for the different people. Replay the video and have students fill in the information. You may want to have students compare their charts with partners. Go over the answers with the whole class to summarize the information.

Sample Answers:
Advantages

For students: can read announcements, find links for research, can continue discussions

For parents: can check grades and homework, can ask teachers questions

For teachers: can answer questions, can be in contact continually

Disadvantages

For students: some may not have Internet access

For parents: parents may try to "micro-manage" their children's studies

For teachers: it is extra work, it takes time to maintain the website

After You Watch

Read the explanation of compound words together. Point out the example and ask volunteers for other examples of compound words that they know, such as: hallway, backpack, bathroom.

Replay the video again and ask students to listen for examples of compound words. Go over the answers together.

Answers:

b. on + line = online

c. web + site = website

d. class + mates = classmates

[Other examples: homework, tonight, anytime, anywhere]

City Life

Goals

- **Read about and discuss city problems and solutions**
- **Use context clues: opposites, examples, explanations**
- **Understand main idea**
- **Understand italics for emphasis**
- **Understand contrast**
- **Make inferences**
- **Summarize**
- **Skim for main ideas**
- **Identify topic and topic sentence**
- **Understand pronoun reference**
- **Classify and evaluate**
- **Understand parts of speech: nouns, verbs, adjectives, adverbs**
- **Scan for information**

Part 1 A City That's Doing Something Right

Before You Read

1 **Discussing Photos. Page 22.**
Ask students to look at the photos on page 22 as you read the questions aloud. Then arrange students in groups of four or five. Give the groups about 10-15 minutes to discuss the questions. Circulate among the groups, listening, and giving assistance as needed. When all groups are finished, ask students to identify and describe the places. As students suggest answers, record students' responses and ideas on an overhead project or on a large piece of paper. You may want to review these responses later after students have read the selection.

Sample Answers:
1. The first picture is probably a poor section of a large city in a developing country. It's a tropical area, maybe in South America or Africa. The second photo looks like an administrative or industrial park in a large city or in a suburban area.

2. Photo 1: crowded, noisy, busy, poor, messy, unsafe, run-down

   Photo 2: clean, quiet, spacious, green, pretty, safe, rich, well-cared for, scenic

3. Some problems might be over-crowding, not enough water, poor transportation system, few jobs, poor sanitation, garbage, poor electrical and phone systems.

2 **Vocabulary Preview. Page 22.**
Read the words aloud and have students check the ones they don't know. Have students check their understanding of the checked words after they complete the reading selection.

3 **Getting Meaning From Context. Page 23.**
As you read the explanations aloud, call attention to each of the examples. Ask students look for the specific words *(for example, for instance, such as, among them; that is, in other words)* in the items in Exercise 3. Review other clues from Chapter 1: parentheses, dashes, commas; logic. Remind students that by using the context clues to guess the meaning of new words, they will increase the speed and efficiency of their reading. Do the first item together as an example. Read the statement aloud and ask volunteers to suggest what the meaning of "predict" is. Then have students complete the exercise individually. If students finish early, they can compare their answers with others in the class. As a group, go over the answers. Encourage volunteers to explain how they developed their definitions.

Answers: 1. tell about the future
2. horrible traffic jams; travel from home to work   3. rich   4. a listing of what is most important   5. garbage   6. potatoes, oranges and other fruits and vegetables   7. a workplace where trash is separated from items that can be reused   8. a system of buses, subways, and other forms of public transportation

Read

4. A City That's Doing Something Right. Page 24. [on tape/CD]

Read the instructions and question aloud. You may want to have students skim to find out what Curitiba is and where it is located. Then, play the tape or CD as students follow along in their books. You may want to stop the recording after every paragraph to check understanding and point out vocabulary words. Listen a second time as students read along.

After You Read

5   Understanding the Main Idea. Page 26.

Review the meaning of "main idea." Then, read the instructions and have students complete the exercise. Discuss the answers with the whole class. You may want to have students correct the false statements to make them true.

Answers: 1. F   2. T   3. F   4. T   5. T

Read the Cross-Cultural Note on Language aloud. Ask students for examples of cognates and false cognates between their native languages and English.

6   Understanding Italics. Page 27.

Read the instructions together. Have students look back at the reading selection on pages 24–26 and find words in italics. You may want to model a few of the sentences for students to listen for the emphasis. Then have students practice reading the sentences in pairs.

7   Understanding Contrast. Page 27.

Read the instructions together, clarifying as needed. Then, allow time for students to look back at the reading to determine the two parts that show that contrast. Go over the answers. Encourage volunteers to point out specific lines and sections that are contrasting.

Sample Answers:
The first part is Paragraph A.
The second part is Paragraphs B–G.

The first part lists common problems of large cities: air pollution, disease, crime, traffic, housing, health care, jobs. The second part shows how the city of Curitiba has solved some of these problems: garbage collection, buses and subways, street children, pollution control.

8   Making Inferences. Page 27.

Go over the instructions together. Remind students that they can look back at the reading to check if the information is stated (so they can find the statements or similar statements in the selection) or if the information is implied (so they can find only some clues to support the statements). Then have students work in pairs or individually to complete the exercise. Go over the answers. Ask volunteers to find and read aloud the statements from the reading that support their answers.

Answers: 1. S   2. I   3. I   4. S   5. S
6. I   7. I   8. S   9. I   10. I

9   Summarizing. Page 27.

After reading the instructions aloud, have students choose the best summary of the reading selection. Go over the answer. Ask volunteers to explain why the other statements are not good summaries.

Answer: 5

10   Page 28.

Ask a volunteer to read the question on page 24 aloud. Then have students work in pairs or individually to prepare an answer. As volunteers read their answers aloud, make notes on the board. Discuss any variations in answers.

Sample Answer:
The city of Curitiba encourages people to get rid of trash in proper places. It has an efficient and effective transportation system. Poor children are given similar jobs in exchange for food and money from local businesses. The city lowers taxes for businesses that make the place beautiful.

Discussing the Reading

11 Small Group Discussion. Page 28.

Arrange students in groups of four. Assign each person in the group a role: 1. reading the questions to the group; 2. restating answers; 3. recording information; 4. reporting the answers to the whole class.

Give the groups about 15-20 minutes to discuss the questions. Circulate among the groups, listening, and giving assistance as need. When all groups are finished, ask the reporters from each group to share the most interesting information from their groups.

Answers will vary.

Part 2 Sick-Building Syndrome

Before You Read

1 Skimming for Main Ideas. Page 28.
Review the meaning of "topic" and "topic sentence" as you read aloud the directions. Remind students that the topic is usually who or what the paragraph is about and the topic sentence is a sentence that gives the general or main idea of the paragraph. Then, have students work individually reading the paragraphs and identifying the topics and topic sentences.

Read

2 Reading for Topics and Topic Sentences. Page 28. [on tape/CD]
Ask students to read the selection again and reconsider their choices of topics and topic sentences. Alternatively, you may want to play the tape or CD again, pausing to ask comprehension questions and pointing out key vocabulary before students look over their answers. After students have checked their own answers, have them complete the After You Read activity.

After You Read

Read the instructions aloud. Then have students exchange and compare their answers. Encourage them to explain their choices to each other. Go over the answers with the whole class.

Sample Answers:
A. Topic: Buildings with indoor air pollution
   Topic sentence: They discovered that St. Charles High, like thousands of other schools and office buildings nationwide, is a "sick building"—in other words, a building that creates its own indoor air pollution.
B. Topic: Pollutants cause disease
   Topic sentence: These pollutants are causing a group of unpleasant and dangerous symptoms that experts call "sick-building syndrome."
C. Topic: Indoor pollution in houses
   Topic sentence: Although most common in office buildings and schools, the indoor pollution that causes sick-building syndrome can also occur in houses.
D. Topic: Bad ventilation in buildings
   Topic sentence: Experts have discovered several sources of sick-building syndrome—among them mold and bacteria, synthetic products, and lack of ventilation—a system of moving fresh air.
E. Topic: Solution by cleaning
   Topic sentence: There are several solutions

to the problem of sick-building syndrome, among them cleansing the building.

F. Topic: Plant solutions
Topic sentence: In another study, scientists found that the chemical interaction among soil, roots, and leaves works to remove pollutants

G. Topic: Questions that remain
Topic sentence: When we are able to answer these questions, we might find that plants offer an important pollution-control system for the 21st century.

3 Understanding Pronoun Reference. Page 31.

Read the instructions aloud before having students complete the exercise. Remind them look back at the reading selection to find the nouns (or nouns phrases) to which the pronouns refer. Go over the answers with the class.

Answers:

1. teachers and students at St. Charles High School
2. people who live in a typical house
3. people who live in a typical house
4. several sources of sick-building syndrome
5. several solutions to the problem of sick-building syndrome
6. workers
7. plants

Discussing the Reading

4 Small Group Discussion. Page 31.

Arrange students in groups of four to discuss their answers to the questions. Give the groups about 15-20 minutes for discussion. As students work, go around listening and assisting as needed. When all groups are finished, invite volunteers to share the most interesting information from their groups.

Talk It Over

Classifying and Evaluating

Read the thoughts of the character in the comic strip aloud. Then, arrange students in groups of four or five to talk about their own thoughts on the comic strip. Allow 15-20 minutes for discussion. As a whole group, summarize the results of the discussions.

Sample Answers:

1. He is worried about indoor pollution and sick-building syndrome.
2. People can become over-worried about the problem. We use many of the different products today in homes. It is almost impossible to avoid all contact with possible sources of indoor pollution.
3. I worry more about air and water pollution more than indoor pollution.
4. Yes, I think some people worry too much. I think they should be realistic that we cannot avoid all possible sources, but we should be careful and try to avoid too many possible problems. People can have their homes checked. They can do simple things like opening windows for a short time every day and make sure things are clean.
5. In the past, sick-building syndrome was not a big problem because we did not use so many synthetic materials. People used to use just natural products. Homes were not so air-tight. People worked more outside than inside buildings, so they spent less time indoors.

Part 3 Building Vocabulary and Study Skills

1 Understanding Parts of Speech (1). Page 32.

Read the instructions aloud and go over the examples clarifying as needed the parts of speech: nouns, verbs. Then, ask students to complete the exercise on their own. Discuss the answers with the whole class.

Answers: 2. crowd (n), crowd (v) 3. answer (v) answer (n) 4. house (n) house (v) 5. increase (v) increase (n) 6. study (n) study (v) 7. worry (v) worry (n) 8. focus (v) focus (n)

2 Understanding Parts of Speech (2). Page 34.

Read the instructions and examples of related words on the chart aloud. Point out common suffixes for nouns and adverbs. Go over the sample together. Then, have students work individually on the exercise. Go over the answers and have students suggest other sentences for the base words.

Answers: 2. pollution (n) pollutant (n) 3. crowd (n) crowded (adj.) 4. safe (adj.) safely (adv.) safety (n) 5. beautiful (adj.) beautify (v) 6. predict (v) worse (adj.) prediction (n) worsen (v) 7. differ (v) difference (n) differently (adv.) different (adj.) 8. efficient (adj.) efficiently (adv.)

3 Looking up Parts of Speech. Page 36.

Read the instructions and explanations aloud. Point out and clarify the various dictionary entry notations and abbreviations. Then have students complete Part A using a dictionary. Go over the answers with the class.

Answers Part A:
2. v, n 3. v, n 4. adj. 5. adj. 6. v, n 7. n 8. v 9. v, n 10. n 11. v, n 12. v, n 13. adj. 14. n 15. adj. 16. v, n

Have students complete Part B with related words. Go over the answers. Ask volunteers to use the related words in sentences to review the functions of the different parts of speech.

Answers Part B:
Nouns: educator, belief, respiration (respirator), tightness

Verbs: educate, infect, originate, respire, tighten

Adjectives: educational, educated, believable, infective (infectious), infected, original, tight

Adverbs: educationally, believably, infectiously (infectively), originally

educate, educational educationally

Focus on Testing

Getting Meaning from Context

Read the instructions together, reminding students of the parts of speech from Exercise 3. Then have students complete the practice test. Remind them that the answer they choose needs to be the same part of speech as the underlined word. Go over the answers with the whole class.

As an extension activity, have students prepare two similar test items using the related words from Exercise 3. Create a practice test for the class using students' test items.

Answers: 1. c, b 2. d 3. c 4. d

Part 4 Reading in the Real World

1 Scanning for Information. Page 38.

Read the instructions aloud and remind students that scanning is examining or reading quickly. Remind them to make use of pictures and subheadings before reading to get a general idea of the topic of the reading selection. Ask volunteers to read the questions aloud. Then tell students to scan the reading and answer the questions. When students are finished, ask volunteers to give their answers. Discuss differences students have in their answers. Encourage students to point out lines from the reading selection where they found the answers.

Sample Answers:
1. Life will be better.
2. People will use cars and trucks less that they do now.
3. There will be fewer toxic chemicals and carcinogens in foods. Fresh produce will be grown locally so transportation will not be a big problem.
4. Shopping malls will be smaller and easier to get to. They will use more natural lights and they will recycle more products.
5. For power sources, people will use windmills and solar panels for generating electricity.

2 Getting Meaning from Context. Page 40.
Have students complete the exercise. Go over the answers together.

Answers: 1. tolerate 2. marathon
3. spewing 4. pristine 5. hop 6. swift
7. in shape 8. markets 9. organic
10. bike racks 11. mammoth 12. flow from
13. solar 14. appliances 15. basement
16. purify

Beyond the Text

Read aloud and discuss the interview questions before assigning this exercise as a homework assignment. Have volunteers report their findings to the class. Encourage students to give their own opinions on the future life. As an extension activity, have students write a composition expressing their own opinions or contrasting different views on future life.

Video Activities: Garbage Car

Before You Watch
Read the questions aloud and ask students to discuss their answers in small groups. Have students report to the class their answers.

Answers will vary.

Watch [on video]
Ask students to read the questions before they view the video. Remind them to watch carefully to find the answers to the questions. Then play the video and have students answer the questions. Review the answers together.

Sample Answers: 1. An abandoned car was left in front of her home. 2. The car smells bad, looks horrible, and is unsafe.
3. Some efforts were made to help her, but the car is still there. 4. She feels frustrated.
5. It's a dangerous situation because the car is a fire hazard and health hazard. It makes people feel depressed.

Watch Again [on video]
Ask students to read the statements. Then, replay the video and have students decide if the statements are true or false. Go over the answers with the whole class. Ask volunteers to restate the false sentences to make them true.

Answers: 1. F 2. T 3. F 4. T 5. T
6. F

After You Watch
Review parts of speech: nouns, verbs, adjectives, adverbs, and prepositions. Ask volunteers to suggest a few examples for each category. Then read aloud the instructions and the list of words. Ask students to raise their hands when they hear one of the words as you replay the video. Pause the video and have volunteers identify the part of speech of the word.

Answers: a. adverb b. noun
c. preposition d. adjective e. noun

Business and Money

Goals

- **Read about and discuss banks and lending organizations**
- **Use context clues: abbreviations**
- **Understand main idea**
- **Understand conclusions**
- **Make inferences**
- **Summarize**
- **Understand irony**
- **Skim for main ideas**
- **Identify topic and topic sentence**
- **Understand pronoun reference**
- **Understand related words**
- **Understand parts of speech: suffixes**
- **Notice phrases**
- **Scan for information**

Part 1 Banking on the Poor

Before You Read

1 **Discussing Photos. Page 44.**

Ask students to look at the photos on page 44. Have volunteers describe the people, places, and activities in the photos. Then arrange students in groups of four or five. Give the groups about 10-15 minutes to discuss the questions which are under the photos. Go around the room helping as needed. When all groups are finished, ask volunteers to share their groups' answers. Record students' responses and ideas on an overhead projector or on a large piece of paper. You may want to review these responses later after students have read the selection.

Sample Answers:

1. In the bank, people might be depositing or withdrawing money, buying money orders, writing out checks, opening bank accounts, paying bills, transferring money, closing accounts, investing money, borrowing money, making payments on loans or mortgages, etc.

2. The people in the other two photos do not need to use banks so much for their small businesses.

3. Some problems they might have are: limited records on their sales and expenses, less secure place for saving their money, difficult to expand their businesses.

2 **Vocabulary Preview. Page 45.**

Read the words aloud and have students check the ones they don't know. Have students check their understanding of the checked words after they complete the reading selection.

3 **Getting Meaning From Context. Page 45.**

As you read the explanations aloud, call attention to each of the abbreviations. Ask students look for the abbreviations in the items in Exercise 3. Have students complete the exercise individually, circling the context clues that help with the meaning and answering the questions. If students finish early, they can compare their answers with others in the class. Go over the answers.

Answers:

1. People who own and run their own small business
   Microentrepreneurs are people who own and run their own small businesses.

2. group members make sure that each person pays back his or her loan
   When there is peer pressure, the group members make sure that other members do what is necessary.

3. violence and lack of education
Some examples of social ills are violence
and lack of education.

4 Context Clues: Related Words. Page 46.

Read the instructions and example together
pointing out the words that are close in meaning
but have different parts of speech. Then have
students complete the exercise. Go over the
answers.

Answers: 1. Noun 2. Honesty 3. Noun
4. Ability to do something

5 Context Clues: Logic. Page 46.

Go over the instructions and example before
asking students to complete the exercise. Review
the answers together.

Answers: 1. verb; raise 2. noun; getting
rid of 3. adjective; smaller 4. noun; amount
of money 5. verb; put, cultivate, invest

Read

6 Banking on the Poor. Page 47.
[on tape/CD]

Read the guiding question in the instructions
aloud. Then, play the tape or CD as students
follow along in their books. You may want to stop
the recording after every paragraph to check
understanding and to point out vocabulary words.
Listen a second time as students read along.

After You Read

7 Getting the Main Ideas. Page 49.

Read the instructions and have students complete
the exercise. Discuss the answers with the whole
class. Ask volunteers to correct the false
statements to make them true.

Answers: 1. T 2. T 3. F 4. T 5. T

8 Understanding Conclusions. Page 49.

Read the instructions together. Then have
students locate the concluding sentence that

refers back to the introduction. Have students
justify their choice.

Answer:
There is hope that they can begin to break the
cycle of poverty for themselves, their families,
and society.

9 Making Inferences. Page 49.

Read the instructions together, clarifying that a
inference is a conclusion or idea that is based on
evidence or stated information. Guide students to
make inferences about changes in a
businesswoman's life. You may want to have
students work in pairs or small groups to
brainstorm ideas. Then ask volunteers to present
their groups' inferences and explain on what facts
they are based.

Sample Answers:
If a woman owns a business, she has choices
and she has to make decisions. So she
becomes more of a leader. She has money, so
she is not dependent on others for financial
support. She has a responsibility to others.

Ask a volunteer to read the question on page
47 aloud. Then have students prepare an
answer. As volunteers read aloud their
answers, make notes on the board. Discuss
any variations in answers.

Sample Answer:
Banks can help poor people to change their
lives by giving them money to start or expand
small businesses. By giving them money to start
a business, the bank shows confidence in the
people. The people have a chance to gains the
respect of others in the community. They can
develop the means to support themselves and
their families.

10 Summarizing. Page 49.

After reading aloud the instructions, have
students choose the best summary of the reading
selection. Go over the answer. Ask volunteers to
explain why the other statements are not good
summaries.

Answer: 3

Discussing the Reading

11 Small Group Discussion. Page 50.

Arrange students in groups of four. Give the groups about 15-20 minutes to discuss the questions. Go around listening and giving assistance as needed. Ask a volunteer from each group to share the most interesting information from their groups.

Answers will vary.

Talk It Over

Understanding Irony

Read the thoughts of the character in the cartoon aloud. Arrange students in groups of four or five to talk about their own thoughts on the cartoon strip. Allow 10-15 minutes for discussion. Ask volunteers from each group to report their ideas. Help summarize the results of the discussions.

Sample Answers:

The cartoonist is saying that people who have money can borrow as much money as they want, but poor people have no right to borrow even a small amount. The rich have no sympathy for those with little or no money.

Part 2 Consumerism and the Human Brain

Before You Read

1 Talk About the Answers. Page 50.

Point out the photo and the title of the reading selection. Then, read the instructions and questions aloud. If needed, show how the photo, title, and questions are related. Arrange students in groups of four or five to share ideas on the pre-reading questions. Allow 10-15 minutes for discussion before asking groups report their ideas. As a whole group, summarize the responses.

Sample Answers:

1. Consumers are people that buy or use things or products.
2. Some people choose a particular brand because of its name, quality, price, convenience, or a personal reason.
3. Advertising influences people because it makes the products seem very attractive and that people need to buy the items. Advertisers use color, names, spokespeople, and imagery to attract customers.
4. A person might choose this brand to be "cool" like the person on the ad.

Read

2 Skimming for Main Ideas. Page 51. [on tape/CD]

Read the directions aloud, reminding students that the topic is usually who or what the paragraph is about and the topic sentence gives the main idea of the paragraph. Then, play the tape or CD as students work individually reading the paragraphs and completing the topics and topic sentences.

After You Read

3 Exchange Answers. Page 54.

Have students exchange and compare their answers to Exercise 2. Encourage them to explain their choices. Allow 10-15 minutes for discussion. Then go over the answers with the whole class.

Sample Answers:

A. Topic: why consumers buy
   Topic sentence: Successful marketers use their knowledge of psychology—and, increasingly, of recent studies of the human brain—to persuade us to consume more and more.

B. Topic: Fear as a motive to buy
   Topic sentence: One way that advertisers persuade us to buy a product is by targeting our dissatisfaction with ourselves, our fears.

C. Topic: Making products attractive
Topic sentence: In a similar way, advertisers also take advantage of our need for a good self-image, our desire to appear attractive, successful, and even exciting.

D. Topic: Smells and preferences
Topic sentence: According to Dr. Alan Hirsch, our sense of smell actually influences our opinion of a product and our decision to buy it.

E. Topic: Persuading us that a product works well
Topic sentence: In marketing, a successful advertisement persuades consumers that a product works well: their belief causes them to use the product in such a way that it does work well.

F. Topic: Marketers affect our thinking
Topic sentence: The truth is, however, that—with their increasing knowledge of what goes on in the human brain—marketers might have more power over us than we realize.

4 Understanding Pronoun Reference. Page 54.
Read the instructions before having students complete the exercise. Go over the answers with the class.

Answers: 1. successful marketers
2. dentists 3. many men 4. a product
5. Dr. Alan Hirsch 6. consumers'

Cross-Cultural Note: Fighting Consumerism
Read the note aloud and have students talk about similar organizations or consumer issues they know.

Discussing the Reading

5 Small Group Discussion. Page 54.
Arrange students in groups of four to discuss their answers to the questions. Give the groups

about 15-20 minutes to discuss the questions. As students are discussing their ideas, go around listening and assisting as needed. When all groups are finished, invite volunteers to share the most interesting information from their groups.

Beyond the Text

Studying Ads
Have students work in groups examining ads that they have found and categorizing them according to the kind of psychology used by the advertisers. Have volunteers from each group, present their ads and justify their categorizations.

Part 3 Building Vocabulary and Study Skills

1 Finding Related Words. Page 55.
Have students complete the exercise on their own, reminding them to cross out the word that does not belong. Discuss the answers with the whole class.

Answers: 2. checks 3. valuable
4. center 5. drive 6. shopping
7. microlending 8. complete 9. accounts
10. claim

2 Understanding Parts of Speech. Page 55.
Read the instructions and point out the common suffixes for nouns and adjectives. You may want to have volunteers suggest words that have these suffixes. Then, have students work individually on the exercise. Go over the answers.

Answers: 3. a 4. n 5. n 6. n 7. a 8. a 9. n 10. n 11. a 12. n 13. n 14. n 15. n 16. n 17. n 18. n 19. a 20. a 21. n 22. n 23. n 24. a 25. n 26. a 27. n 28. a/n 29. n 30. a 31. a 32. a 33. n

3 Using Related Words. Page 56.
Have students complete the exercise individually.
Go over the answer together.

Answers: 1. marketer, consumer
2. violent, offensive   3. information, influence
4. successful, society

Focus on Testing

Paying Attention to Phrases
Read the instructions and examples together. You
may want to demonstrate or have students
identify some noun, verb, prepositional, and
infinitive phrases in the first paragraph of the
instructions. Point out that by reading in phrases,
you will be able to understand the meaning more
easily than if you were reading word by word.

4 Understanding Phrases. Page 57.
Answers:

(prep.)
For many people, there seems to be no
(verb)   (prep.)
escape from poverty; in other words, they are
(verb)
poor, and they have no hope that this will ever
(prep)   (noun)
change. In addition, they have the social
(noun)   (verb)
problems of poverty. Imagine this situation;
(noun)   (verb)   (noun)
a poor woman has an idea for a small business
(prep.)
to lift herself and her family out of poverty.
(noun)   (infinitive)
She needs a little money to begin this business.
(verb)   (infinitive)
She goes to a bank to borrow the money,
(prep.)
and the banker interviews her. At this bank,
(verb)
as at most banks, the borrower must meet three
(verb)
necessary conditions: character, capacity, and
collateral. That is, if this woman wants
(infinitive)   (prep.)

to borrow money from the bank, she must show
(verb)
that she (1) is honest (has character), (2) is able
(infinitive)
to run her business (has capacity), and
(verb)
(3) owns a house, land, or something valuable
(collateral) for the bank to take if she
(verb)
can't pay back the money. So what happens to
(verb)
the woman? The bank won't lend her the money

because she doesn't have any collateral.
(prep.)
In such a situation, there seems to be no way
(infinitive)
for the woman to break the cycle of poverty.

5 Recognizing Phrases. Page 58.
Assign this as homework. Then in class, have pairs
of students compare their underlined phrases.
Encourage students to read some of their
sentences aloud to hear if their word groups and
phrases make sense. Discuss any differences in
phrases.

Answers will vary.

Part 4 Reading in the Real World

1 Scanning for Information. Page 59.
Read the instructions aloud and remind students
that scanning is examining or reading quickly. Tell
students to highlight important information that
answers the question about a healthy life.

2 Comparing Answers. Page 60.
When students are finished scanning, ask them to
compare their highlighted versions with a
partner's version. Tell them to discuss any
differences students in their markings.

Sample Answers:
Paragraph B: heredity; reduce its negative
effect; optimize its benefits

Paragraph C: Avoiding smoking or tobacco products

Paragraph D: A positive attitude

Paragraph E: A diet low in red meat and other saturated fats and high in complex carbohydrates

Paragraph F: learn about good health, diet and stress management

Paragraph G: Getting annual physicals

Paragraph H: Relaxing regularly; laughing

3 Getting Meaning from Context. Page 60.
Have students complete the exercise. Together, go over the answers.

Answers: 1. up front 2. optimists
3. pessimists 4. likelihood 5. costly
6. annual 7. physicals 8. disorders
9. strengthen 10. "make ends meet"

Beyond the Text

Read aloud and discuss the interview instructions. You may want to have students survey another class or survey a group of friends. Allow time in class for students to work in groups to compare their results and develop some conclusions about the importance of each of the items. Ask volunteers from each group to share their conclusions.

Video Activities: A Teenage Stockbroker

Before You Watch
Read the questions aloud and ask students to discuss their answers in small groups. Have students report to the class their answers.

Sample Answers:
1. Investments in companies and businesses. They are papers that show partial

ownership in a company's profits and losses.
2. A place where stocks and bonds are bought and sold.
3. Puts (invests) money in stocks, businesses, or property to earn interest or make a profit.
4. A possibility of losing money if things go badly.

Watch [on video]
Ask students to read the questions before they view the video. Then play the video and have them answer the questions. Review the answers together.

Sample Answers:
1. Dan is 17 years old. He's a millionaire.
2. He's standing at NASDAQ at the New York Stock Exchange.

Cultural Note:
NASDAQ means National Association of Securities Dealers Automated Quotation system.

Watch Again [on video]
Ask students to read the statements. Then, replay the video and have students decide if the statements are true or false. Go over the answers with the whole class. Ask volunteers to restate the false sentences to make them true.

Answers: 1. T 2. F 3. F 4. F 5. T

After You Watch
Bring in investment sections and/or have students find websites with stock quotations and investment news. If possible, have them compare and contrast how the stock information is presented. Then have students talk about the answers to the questions about companies listed and quantity and value of stocks.

Answers will vary.

Jobs and Professions

Goals

- **Read about and discuss career trends**
- **Use context clues and logic**
- **Understand main idea**
- **Understand the prefix:** *over-*
- **Understand important details**
- **Skim for main ideas**
- **Identify topic and topic sentence**
- **Understand pronoun reference**
- **Understand proverbs and quotations**
- **Understand adjective and noun phrases**
- **Understand compound words**
- **Increase reading speed**
- **Scan for information**

Part 1 Changing Career Trends

Before You Read

1 **Discussing Photos. Page 64.**

Ask students to look at the photos on page 64. Have volunteers describe the people, places, and activities in the photos. Arrange students in groups of four or five to discuss the questions which are under the photos. Then, ask volunteers to share their groups' answers. Have them point out specific clues in the photos that support their answers.

Sample Answers:

1. The first photo was taken in the 1950s. The man is sitting behind his desk in his office. He's reviewing some papers or letters or giving his secretary some work to do.

2. The second photo was taken in the 1990s or later. The woman is sitting at her computer. She is looking at someone or something.

3. Work has changed a lot with many modern office machines: fax machines, computers, Internet, e-mail, copiers, network systems, many computer programs for accounting, bookkeeping, drawing, publishing, etc. Dress and behavior are more casual now.

4. Answers will vary.

2 **Vocabulary Preview. Page 64.**

Read the words aloud and have students check the ones they don't know. After they have completed the reading selection exercises, have them look back at this list to check their understanding of the new words.

Read

3 **Changing Career Trends. Page 65. [on tape/CD]**

As you read the instructions aloud, call attention to the question: What are some ways in which work is changing? Remind students to use this question to help guide their reading of the selection. Play the tape or CD and have students follow along in their books. You may want to pause the recording occasionally to check understanding and point out vocabulary words. Listen a second time as students read along.

After You Read

4 **Getting the Main Ideas. Page 67.**

Read the instructions and have students complete the exercise. Discuss the answers with the whole class. Ask volunteers to correct the false statements to make them true.

Answers: 1. √ 2. — 3. — 4. √ 5. √ 6. √ 7. — 8. √ 9. — 10. —

5 Getting Meaning from Context. Page 67.

Go over the instructions and example before asking students to complete the exercise. Review the answers together.

Answers:
1. A livelihood is a job that allows a person make enough money to live.
2. A post is a job.
3. Secure means constant, stable, or safe.
4. Self-confidence is a belief in your own ability.
5. If you upgrade your skills it means that you improve them or you learn something new.
6. To keep up with the field is to continue to make advances and to learn more about what is new.
7. Telecommuting is communicating by computer.
8. To distract is to keep someone from focusing or paying attention.
9. A drawback is a disadvantage.
10. Leisure activities are activities you do when you are relaxing and not working.
11. Ulcers are an example of physical symptoms.

6 Scanning for Words. Page 68.

Have students complete the exercise individually. Then, go over the answers.

Answers: 1. career counselors 2. varies 3. job security 4. unemployment rate 5. job hopping

7 Using the prefix *over-*. Page 69.

Read the explanation and example together. Then tell students to complete the exercise individually. As you go over the answers, ask volunteers to use the new words in sentences.

Answers: 1. overdo 2. overcrowded 3. overestimate 4. overdue 5. overpopulation

8 Different Terms. Page 69.

Read the information about cell phones together. If students are not familiar with cell phones, bring in brochures and advertisements about them or have students look on the Internet for companies that produce and sell cell phones.

9 Understanding Details. Page 69.

Ask students to answer the questions about the reading. When they are finished, have them compare answers with a partner. If they don't agree on an answer, have them look back in the reading.

Sample Answers:
1. The lack of job security can cause worry, depression, and a lack of self-confidence.
2. People that want to keep their jobs or find better jobs should upgrade their skills.
3. One advantage of telecommuting is that the worker can set his or her own work time. (Or the worker needs to spend less time commuting in traffic.) One disadvantage is that it is often hard to focus on work at home because of all the distractions.
4. An advantage to using cell phones and beepers is that you can be in touch with people all the time. A disadvantage is that it is hard to separate work from the rest of your life.
5. Workaholism is a problem when the person overworks and doesn't enjoy the work. The worker has no time to relax so he or she might get sick or depressed. It's not a problem if the person likes the work and feels good about it.

10 Understanding Main Ideas. Page 70.

After reading the instructions aloud, have students choose the main idea of the reading selection. Go over the answer. Ask volunteers to explain why the other statements are not the main idea.

Answer: 5

11 Checking Your Understanding. Page 70.

After reading the instructions aloud, have students answer the question on page 65. Ask volunteers to share their answers. Talk about any differences in the answers

Sample Answer:

Work is changing in many ways. People don't have the same job security, so workers need to be more flexible and always ready to learn new skills and information. Modern technology makes it possible for workers to work at home and communicate through computers. Workers need to be able to separate work from leisure to avoid stress-related problems.

Discussing the Reading

12 Small Group Discussion. Page 70.

Arrange students in groups of five or six. Give the groups about 15-20 minutes to discuss the questions. Go around listening and giving assistance as needed. Ask a volunteer from each group to share the most interesting information from their groups.

Answers will vary.

Part 2 Looking for Work in the Twenty-First Century

Before You Read

1 Thinking Ahead. Page 70.

Arrange students in small groups to discuss the answers to the questions about preparing for and searching for jobs. Ask a volunteer from each group to share their responses. Guide students to make predictions about the next reading selection based on the questions they just answered and the title of Part 2.

Answers will vary.

Read

2 Skimming for Main Ideas. Page 70. [on tape/CD]

Read the directions aloud, reviewing what a topic and topic sentence are. Then, have students work individually reading the paragraphs and identifying the topics and topic sentences. You may play the selection on the tape or CD and have students follow along in their books.

After You Read

3 Checking Your Answers. Page 73.

Have students exchange and compare their answers to Exercise 2. Encourage them to explain their choices to each other. Allow 10-15 minutes for discussion. Then go over the answers with the whole class.

Sample Answers:

A. Topic: Looking for a job in the past
   Topic sentence: Not very long ago, when people needed to find a job, there were several possible steps.

B. Topic: First steps in current job hunting
   Topic sentence: The first step is to determine what kind of job you want (which sounds easier than it is) and make sure that you have the right education for it.

C. Topic: Career counseling advice
   Topic sentence: All career counselors— private or public—agree on one basic point: it is important for people to find a career that they love.

D. Topic: The Internet and Job hunting
   Topic sentence: The biggest change in job hunting these days is the use of the Internet.

E. Topic: Applying for a job on the Internet
   Topic sentence: A job seekers can reply to a "Help Wanted" notice on a company's website.

4 Understanding Pronoun Reference. Page 73.

Have students complete the exercise. Go over the answers with the class.

Answers: 1. people looking for a job 2. the kind of job you want   3. their dream job   4. job boards   5. job interview and skills test   6. job hunting

Discussing the Reading

5 Small Group Discussion. Page 73.

Arrange students in groups of four to discuss their answers to the questions. Give the groups about 15-20 minutes to discuss the questions. As students are discussing their ideas, go around listening and assisting as needed. When all groups are finished, invite volunteers to share the most interesting information from their groups.

Talk It Over

Understanding Proverbs and Quotations

Go over the instructions clarifying what a proverb is. Read aloud the proverbs and quotations. Then, arrange students in groups of four or five to talk about their own thoughts on the meaning of the proverbs and quotations. Allow 15-20 minutes for discussion. Ask groups to share their explanations.

Sample Answers:
1. There needs to be a balance between work and relaxation. Too much work is not good for a person.
2. You need to work hard to think of good, creative ideas.
3. People work slowly if they have plenty of time, but they can do the same work in a much shorter time if they have to.
4. If a person is lazy, then they will be poor. A person who works will become successful.

5. If you like your work, you will be happy. Being rich or famous does not bring happiness.

Beyond the Text

Finding Ads on the Internet

If students are interested, have them check some of the site for job postings. Students can share what information and opportunities they found on the web.

Part 3 Building Vocabulary and Study Skills

1 Adjective and Noun Phrases. Page 75.

Read the explanation aloud. Call attention to the examples of adjective and noun phrases. Ask students for other examples. Then have students complete the exercise on their own. Discuss the answers with the whole class.

Answers: 1. dream   2. unemployment, part, self   3. city, shopping, mass, traffic   4. career, computer   5. job, personnel

2 Pairs of Words. Page 76.

Students can complete the exercise individually. Then go over the answers with the class.

Answers: 2. a 3. h 4. e 5. b 6. g 7. c 8. f

3 Compound Words. Page 76.

Review the meaning of "compound words." Ask volunteers for some examples. Then have students match the compound words with their meanings in the exercise. Go over the answer together. You may want to have volunteers use the compound words in sentences to illustrate their meanings.

Answers: 2. e 3. j 4. a 5. i 6. b 7. c 8. f 9. d 10. g

4 Compound Words and Phrases. Page 77.

You may want to have students work in pairs or small groups to compile lists for this activity. Go over the answers by having a volunteer read his or her list. Others should check off the words that are the same. Then ask others to name additional words from their lists.

Sample Answers:
High school, high life, high security, security department

Science lab, science exam, science department

Lab work, computer lab

Office work, office computer, office network, public network, city network, job network

College exam, college life, college tuition, city college

Self-exam, self-service, self-confidence

Office website, school website, city website

Life work, job life, school life, city life

Public work, school work, city work, security work, computer work

College exam, security exam

Public school, public service, public job

School interview, security interview, job interview

School tuition, tuition planning

City school, school security, school department, school planning

Computer service

City job, city planning

Network security, market security, job security, computer security

Job market, job confidence, computer job, job planning

Focus on Testing

Increasing Reading Speed—Left-to-Right Eye Movement

Read the instructions together pointing out that students are reading to find the same words. Time

students as they complete each of the sections. At the end of each section, stop and have students count and check the number of words they underlined in each line.

Answers:
banking 3
challenge 2
savings 2
benefit 2
employer 0

experience 2
opening 2
excellent 3
identify 2
account 3

part-time 2
position 2
public 2
appointment 1
personnel 1

salary 1
apply 3
pleasure 1
skills 2
ability 2

Part 4 Reading in the Real World

1 Vocabulary Preview. Page 79.

Have students complete the vocabulary exercise. Point out that they can use a dictionary. Go over the answers and have volunteers model using the vocabulary words in sentences.

Answers: 2. c 3. e 4. a 5. j 6. f
7. i 8. b 9. h 10. k 11. d

2 Preparing to Read. Page 79.

Read the explanations and instructions aloud. Call attention to the chart in Exercise 3. Tell students to use the questions on the chart to guide them as they read and mark up the reading selection. After students have completed the reading, you may want to have them compare the information that they marked.

3 Scanning for Information. Page 80.

Have students complete the chart, referring back to the reading and their markings as needed. Together, go over the answers.

Answers:

1st Period

Years: 1455-1571

1. invention of printing press
2. Renaissance
3. European discovery of America
4. reawakening of science
5. Protestant Reformation

2nd Period

Years: 1776-1815

3. Industrial Revolution
4. public school system founded
5. modern universities started: Berlin
6. capitalism and communism as economic and political ideologies

3rd Period

Years: 1960-now

1. introduction of computer
2. emergence of Japan as global economic power

4 Checking Your Understanding. Page 81.

Have students look for more details in the reading selection and answer the questions. Discuss students' answers.

Sample Answers:

1. We are living in the post-capitalist era.

2. Knowledge will be the basis of wealth in the new society. Labor or work will not be the basis of wealth.

3. There will be two groups of workers: knowledge workers and service workers.

4. There might be class conflict if the service workers feel that they are socially and economically disadvantaged.

Video Activities: I Love My Job

Before You Watch

Read the questions aloud and ask students to discuss their answers in small groups. Have students report to the class their answers.

Answers will vary.

Watch [on video]

Ask students to read the questions before they view the video. Then play the video. You may want to have students discuss their answers in small groups or have a large class discussion.

Sample Answers:

1. Lu is slight, well dressed, and well groomed. Her white hair is styled, and she wears glasses. She is happy and friendly. She's probably in her seventies.

2. Customers like her because she is so happy and friendly all the time. She also knows all the customers' names and remembers what they order.

3. Lu loves her job and customers.

4. Nicolosi's restaurant is probably an Italian family restaurant.

Watch Again [on video]

Ask students to read these questions. Then, replay the video and have students respond to the questions. Go over the answers with the whole class.

Sample Answers:

1. Luella has a good memory and she has an optimistic personality.

2. "To kill people with kindness" means to be nice and kind to others and eventually bad or mean people will be nice back.

3. Answers will vary.

4. She probably is still working because she loves the work and the people. They are important to her.

After You Watch

Students can work in pairs to complete the exercise. As you go over the answers, encourage students to share any experience they have had eating or preparing any of the dishes. If possible, bring in some sample Italian menus for students to look at.

Sample Answers:

a. pizza: a type of bread crust in a small baking pan topped with tomato sauce, cheese, and maybe other toppings.

b. pepperoni: very spicy, dry meat sausage.

c. ravioli: a square-shaped pasta filled with cheese or other filling and served with sauce.

d. spaghetti: long strings of pasta that are boiled and then served with sauce.

e. lasagna: flat wide pasta that is arranged in a baking pan in layers with tomato sauce, cheese, and other fillings.

Lifestyles Around the World

Goals

- **Read about and discuss fashion trends**
- **Understand main idea**
- **Use context clues to make inferences**
- **Classify trends**
- **Mark a book for skimming**
- **Summarize**
- **Recognize stereotypes**
- **Understand prefixes and suffixes**
- **Understand dictionary entries**
- **Scan scientific articles**
- **Take multiple-choice tests**

Part 1 Trendspotting

Before You Read

1 Getting Started. Page 84.

Ask students to look at the pictures on page 84. Have volunteers describe the people, time periods, and activities. Then arrange students in groups of four or five to discuss the questions. Allow about 10-15 minutes, then ask volunteers to share their groups' answers. Record key vocabulary and ideas on the board or on a large piece of paper for reference.

Sample Answers:

1. In the first picture, the people are wearing T-shirts, jeans, (saddle) shoes and crew socks. In the background, a girl is wearing a poodle skirt. The boy and girl are sharing a drink. Another girl is playing with a hula hoop.

   In the second picture, the people are wearing bell-bottom pants, beads, hippie clothes. The "Beatles" are singing. The girl is carrying a guitar and making a peace sign. The others are sitting and meditating.

   In the last picture, the boy is wearing baggy clothes: jeans and T-shirt and he has an earring. The woman is wearing a business suit. There are people in-line skating, talking on a cell phone, using a laptop computer, and jogging.

2. In the first picture, there is a large car in front of a drive-in hamburger place. It was a common place for young people to hang-out in the 50s. Elvis Presley is pictured. He was a popular singer at that time.

   In the second picture, the Beatles were popular at that time. Many people had long hair.

3. The first picture is probably during the 50s. The second one is from the 60s. The last one is 1990s-present time.

4. Answers will vary.

2 Vocabulary Preview. Page 85.

Have students check the words they don't know as you read the words aloud. Ask them to look back at this list later after they have completed the reading selection exercises to check their understanding of the words.

Read

3 Trendspotting. Page 85. [on tape/CD]

As you read the instructions aloud, call attention to the question: *What are fads and trends, and why are they important?* Explain that students should think about this question as they read to help them focus on the main ideas and important details. Play the tape or CD and have students follow along in their books. Stop the recording occasionally to check understanding and to point out vocabulary words. Play the tape or CD a second time as needed.

After You Read

4 Getting the Main Ideas. Page 87.

Ask students to complete the exercise. Then discuss the answers with the whole class. Encourage volunteers to correct the false statements to make them true.

Answers: 1. T 2. T 3. F 4. F 5. T
6. T

5 Getting Meaning from Context. Page 87.

Go over the instructions. Clarify as needed by doing the first item together. Have volunteers find the word "lifestyles" in Paragraph A of the reading selection. Read the first and second sentence aloud. Then, model making inferences or guesses about the meaning of "lifestyles" based on the information in the sentences. Students can work individually or in pairs to complete the exercise. Go over the answers together. Encourage volunteers to explain how they arrived at their definitions.

Answers:

1. ways of living
2. popular interests that are short-lived and not very important
3. central quality or main point
4. money
5. fad language; popular words
6. a longer-lasting popularity of something
7. ability to identify a trend early
8. an advantage
9. tell the difference between
10. register for or sign up for something

6 Check Your Understanding. Page 88.

Have students complete the exercise individually. Then, go over the possible answers.

Sample Answer:

A fad is something that many people do for a brief time. They do it because it is popular idea at the time. A trend is a popular idea for a longer period of time. Fads and trends are important because people in business can develop companies or products that can make a large profit.

7 Understanding Main Ideas. Page 88.

Ask students to read the statements and choose the best statement of the main idea. As you go over the answers, ask volunteers to explain why the other choices are not good summaries of the main idea.

Answer: 5

Discussing the Reading

8 Small Group Discussion. Page 88.

Allow time for students to complete the chart individually. Point out that some categories may have several items and others might have only one or two. Students may want to look through current magazines or just to observe people to see if they can identify some current fads or trends. Then arrange students in groups of five or six to compare their charts. Ask a volunteer from each group to share the most interesting items from their groups discussions.

Answers will vary.

Part 2 Fads and Trends at the Turn of the Twenty-First Century

Before You Read

1 Marking a Book for Skimming. Page 89. [on tape/CD]

Read the directions aloud, reviewing definitions of *topic, main ideas,* and *details,* as needed. Call attention to Paragraph A which has already been marked. Comment on the various phrases that are underlined and why they are important. Then have students work individually on reading the other paragraphs and marking the important information. You may choose to play the tape or CD as students read. Have students summarize the topic and topic sentence for each paragraph.

Encourage them to explain their choices to each other. Allow 10-15 minutes for discussion. Go over the answers with the whole class.

Sample Answers:

B. Topic: Indian fads
Topic sentence: Mehndi (painting designs on hands and neck) and using bidis (candy-flavored cigarettes) are popular fads from India.

C. Topic: Scent and aromatherapy
Topic sentence: Scents are used to make people feel more relaxed, alert, or awake.

D. Topic: Extreme sports
Topic sentence: People who want thrills do dangerous sports, such as sky-surfing and waterfall running, to make themselves feel more alive.

Sample Answers:

Paragraph B: Some current fashion fads come India. Mehndi is a way of painting designs on the body. They are temporary in contrast to tattooing. Bidis are candy-flavored cigarettes that are becoming popular. These bidis have nicotine like regular cigarettes, so it is not a good fad.

Paragraph C: Aromatherapy, or using scents, is used to make people feel different ways. Scents from flowers and lemon, pine, and mint make you feel better. Some scents can make you feel more relaxed. Others make you feel awake and alert.

Paragraph D: Extreme sports are popular among some people. They have changed some regular sports into more dangerous ones. Sky-surfing is a combination of sky-diving and surfing. Waterfall-running is riding a kayak through waterfalls. The people who do these sports like the thrills and danger. The sports make them feel more alive.

After You Read

2 Learning to Summarize. Page 91.
Read the explanation and sample summaries aloud. Guide students to notice similarities and differences between the two sample summaries.

3 Comparing Markings. Page 91.
Arrange students in small groups to compare their markings of Paragraphs B, C, and D. Remind them that their marking may vary, but there should be general agreement on most of the important details.

4 Writing a Summary. Page 91
You may want to assign specific paragraphs for students to summarize. Students may want to work in pairs to prepare their summaries. Students can compare their summaries in small groups. Tell them to check for overall agreement of main idea and important details.

Discussing the Reading

5 Small Group Discussion. Page 92.
Arrange students in groups of four to answers to the questions. Allow about 15-20 minutes for the group discussions. During the group activity, go around listening and assisting as needed. When all groups are finished, invite volunteers to share the most interesting responses and ideas from their groups.

Answers will vary.

Cross-Cultural Note: Fads in Korea
Read and discuss the fads. Have students consider which ones they think are good and might last and which ones might disappear quickly. Allow students to share any fads or trends that are popular in their communities.

Talk It Over

Breaking Stereotypes

Read the instructions together clarifying what stereotypes are. Call attention to the list of stereotypes on page 93. Then, arrange students in groups of four or five to discuss their own thoughts on the specific stereotypes mentioned in the statements. Students can complete the chart activity comparing stereotypes that people make of their culture and stereotypes of another culture. Ask volunteers to share some of the ideas from their charts. As an extension, you may want to have students write a composition comparing the stereotypes based on the information on their charts.

Answers will vary.

Part 3 Building Vocabulary and Study Skills

1 Suffixes and Prefixes. Page 94.

Read the explanation aloud. Ask students to look back on page 55 for the list of previously studied suffixes and prefixes. Have volunteers suggest nouns that end with the new suffixes: -ess, -ship, -ism; -ate, -ize, -en; -less; -ly. Ask others to use the words to sentences to review the function of nouns, verbs, adjectives, and adverbs. Then have students complete the exercise. Go over the answers with the class.

Answers: 1. n 2. n 3. n 4. adj.
5. adj. 6. n 7. n 8. adj. 9. adj. or n
10. adj. 11. n 12. n 13. n 14. adv.
15. v 16. adv. 17. n 18. v 19. n 20. v
21. n 22. n or v 23. n 24. adj. 25. adj.
26. adj. 27. n 28. v 29. adj. 30. adv.
31. n 32. v 33. adj. 34. adv. 35. adj.
36. adj.

2 Prefixes. Page 94.

After you read together the explanation and instructions, call attention to the example and list of common prefixes that mean "no" and "not." You

may want to have volunteers suggest some words that begin with these prefixes. Then have students complete the exercise individually, using a dictionary as needed. Go over the answers, asking volunteers to use the new words in sentences.

Answers: 3. in- 4. un- 5. un- 6. ir-
7. un- 8. in- 9. un- 10. dis- 11. im-
12. un-

3 Other Prefixes. Page 95.

Point out the prefixes and meanings. Have volunteers suggest some examples of words with these prefixes. Then tell students to complete the exercise individually. Review the answers with the whole class. You may want to have volunteers use the words in sentences to illustrate their meanings.

Answers: 1. g 2. i 3. c 4. a 5. j
6. b 7. e 8. d 9. h 10. f

4 Dictionary Entries. Page 96.

Review abbreviations and parts of a dictionary entry by having students look up specific words in a dictionary. Be sure they can find the part of speech, pronunciation, meanings, and examples. Then have students complete the exercise individually or in pairs.

Answers: 1. verb 2. to make (oneself or another person) officially a member of a group, school, etc. 3. enrollment 4. noun
5. a short-lived interest or practice

5 Dictionary Entries with More Than One Meaning. Page 96.

Read the instructions and example together. Be sure students can find the different meanings of the word "style." Then have students complete the exercise.

Answers: 1. noun; I don't like the current style of shoes. 2. 5; 1 3. noun; noun; verb
4. a. in a grand way; b. general way of doing something; c. formed in a certain pattern, shape, etc.; d. fashion, especially in clothes

6 More Dictionary Entries. Page 97.

Go over the instructions before having students complete the exercise. Go over the answers with the group.

Answers: 1. Noun, a dirty mark; verb, pick out with the eye; recognize;   2. Adjective, quick to see and act; watchful; verb, to warn   3. Verb, to consider to be of great worth; noun, the worth of something in money or as compared with other goods for which it might be changed; noun, worth compared with the amount paid   4. Noun, a strong upright pole or bar made of wood, metal, etc.; verb, to make public or show by fixing to a wall, board, post, etc.

Part 4 Reading in the Real World

1 Scanning Scientific Articles. Page 99.

After you read the explanation together, have students read and complete the test individually. Remind them of the test-taking tips above. Go over the answers with the class. You may want to have students point out the lines from the reading to support the answers.

Answers: 1. e   2. e   3. b   4. b   5. a   6. e

Video Activities: Telecommuting

Before You Watch

Read the questions aloud and ask students to discuss their answers in small groups. Have students report to the class their answers.

Answers will vary.

Watch [on video]

Ask students to read the questions before they view the video. Then play the video. You may want to have students discuss their answers in small groups or have a large class discussion.

Sample Answers: 1. David Carroll changed his work hour to avoid a lot of traffic. He goes to work very early and leaves to go home early.   2. Marty Barrazo works at home.

Watch Again [on video]

Ask students to read the statements and decide if they are true or false. Then, replay the video and have students check their responses. Go over the answers with the whole class.

Answers: 1. F   2. T   3. T   4. F   5. F   6. T   7. F

After You Watch

Call attention to the sample combined words and words with prefixes. Then have students complete the exercise in small groups. As you go over the groups' words, encourage volunteers to use the words in sentences and to explain the meanings of the words.

Answers will vary.

Global Connections

Goals

- **Read about and discuss global trade**
- **Understand main idea**
- **Understand figurative meanings**
- **Understand outlines**
- **Make inferences**
- **Skim for main ideas**
- **Understand idioms**
- **Summarize**
- **Use present and past participles**
- **Increase reading speed**
- **Scan for information**

Part 1 Global Trade

Before You Read

1 Getting Started. Page 106.

Call attention to the pictures on page 106. Have volunteers describe the activities and work settings. Then arrange students in groups of four or five to discuss the questions. After 10-15 minutes, have volunteers report their groups' answers. Record key vocabulary and ideas on the board or on a large piece of paper for reference.

Sample Answers:

1. Some reasons for economic success might be industrialization, transportation, modernization, and financial resources.

2. Some reasons for economic failure might be lack of industry or resources, no centralized efficient transportation, lack of financial resources.

3. The workers with the highest yearly income would probably be in Hong Kong and in the modern offices and factories.

4. Geography can help an economy if the land is located near a large river or ocean for easy transportation. It can hurt if the land is not easy to develop, does not have resources, or does not allow efficient transportation systems.

2 Vocabulary Preview. Page 107.

Have students check the ones they don't know as you read aloud the words..

Read

3 Global Trade. Page 107. [on tape/CD]

Call attention to the guiding question in the instructions. Explain that students should think about this question as they read to help them focus on the main ideas and important details. Play the tape or CD and have students follow along in their books. Pause the recording to check understanding and to point out vocabulary words as needed. Then listen a second time.

After You Read

4 Getting the Main Ideas. Page 109.

After students complete the exercise, discuss the answers. Ask volunteers to correct the false statements to make them true.

Answers: 1. T 2. F 3. T 4. F 5. T

5 Getting Meaning from Context. Page 109.

Go over the instructions and example. Be sure students understand the difference between literal and figurative meanings. After students complete the exercise, go over the answers together.

Answers: 1. d 2. a 3. c 4. d 5. b 6. d 7. e 8. d 9. c

6 Find Words and Expressions. Page 111.

Have students complete the exercise individually. Then, go over the possible answers.

Answers: 1. benefits 2. which in turn 3. consumers 4. products or goods 5. fuel 6. reduce 7. harbor 8. tide 9. gap 10. widening 11. landlocked 12. nutrients 13. obstacle 14. it goes without saying 15. protectionist policies 16. subsidy 17. unlike 18. infrastructure

7 Checking Your Understanding. Page 112.

After students answer the question, invite volunteers to share their responses. Discuss differences in the answers.

Sample Answer:

The main key to a country's economic success seems to be open trade. Open trade brings more competition, more choice, and better prices for developed countries. It brings key goods and materials for developing countries.

8 Understanding Outlines. Page 112.

Call attention to the outline in Exercise 8 as you read the instructions together. Point out the format and organization of ideas. Students can work in pairs reading the outline and answering the questions about it. Go over the answers together.

Answers:
1. The topic of the outline is the benefits of open trade
2. Three benefits of open trade for developed countries are competition, lower prices, and more consumer choices.
3. Two problems with the idea that "the rising tide lifts all the boats" is that some "boats" are leaking (and sinking lower) and this makes the gap between the rich and poor countries wider.
4. Two examples of protectionist policies are agricultural subsidies and "hidden" protectionist policies such as health and safety standards.

5. Two ways that government policies can help people in poor countries are infrastructure (transportation and communication systems) and education.

9 Identifying the Main Idea. Page 113.

Have students choose the main idea. Go over the correct answer and have volunteers explain why the other statements are not the main idea.

Answer: 5

10 Page 113.

You may want to have students discuss this question in pairs or small groups before having volunteers give their opinions. Prepare a chart to record students' opinions on the writer's purpose and viewpoint.

Answers will vary.

Discussing the Reading

11 Small Group Discussion. Page 113.

Arrange students in groups of five or six to answer the questions about economic conditions in their countries. Ask a volunteer from each group to share the most interesting items from their groups discussions.

Answers will vary.

Focus on Testing

Making Inferences

After reading the instructions and example together, have volunteers point out specific words and expressions that can be used to make the inference. Then have students complete the exercise. Remind students to look back at the reading selection on pages 107-108 to verify their answers. Go over the answers together.

Answers: 1. a, c 2. a, b, e 3. b, c, d 4. a, c, e

Part 2 Global Travel ... and Beyond

1 Skimming for Main Ideas. Page 115. [on tape/CD]

Read the directions aloud, reminding students that skimming is reading quickly to get the main idea. Have students complete the exercise. You may also play the tape or CD as students read. Go over the answers together.

Answers: A. 2 B. 4 C. 1 D. 3
E. 5 F. 5

After You Read

2 Understanding Idioms. Page 119.

Read the explanation and example aloud. Remind students to use context clues and logic to guess the meanings of the idioms. Students can complete the exercise individually or in pairs. As you go over the answers together, ask volunteers to use the idioms in their own sentences.

Answers: 1. hold people back   2. on your own   3. on the market for   4. getting from one place to another   5. on board
6. private eye   7. track down   8. whodunit
9. pulled into   10. rough it   11. get around
12. sign up for   13. take their time

3 Making Inferences. Page 120.

Review making inferences before having students complete the exercise. Remind students to look back at the reading selection to find the appropriate information. Go over the answers with the group.

Answers:
Paragraph A: 2. √ They think of expensive cruise ships. 3. √ These days there is an enormous variety of possibilities. 4. —

Paragraph B: 1. √ Now, for people with money, it can also offer education or adventure. 2. — 3. — 4. √ For people who

are looking for fun and adventure, there is the Mystery Express.

Paragraph C: 1. √ Perhaps then, it is fortunate that there is a growing interest in ecotourism. 2. — 3. √ Serious ecotourists are interested in preserving the environment and learning about wildlife. 4. √ Many travelers choose to rough it.

Paragraph D: 1. — 2. — 3. But for those who don't have a lot of money for tuition, volunteering for a few weeks can also offer a rich learning experience. 4. √ Volunteering for a few weeks can also offer a rich learning experience.

Paragraph E: 1. √ People who enjoy ocean travel but don't have money for a cruise ship... 2. √ but don't have money for a cruise ship might try a freighter. 3. — 4. √ For people who want to take their time, it's a relaxing way to travel.

Paragraph F: 1. √ By this idiom, they mean, of course.... Will soon be able to use this expression *literally*... 2. — 3. √ The price might be an obstacle. 4. —

4 Summarizing. Page 122.

You may want to assign specific paragraphs for students to summarize. Later, have students who wrote summaries of the same paragraphs compare their summaries in small groups. Tell them to check for overall agreement of main idea and important details.

Sample Answers:
Paragraph A: Global travel used to be expensive. Now people can travel cheaply and take advantage of many different types of travel possibilities.

Paragraph B: People can learn as they travel by train. Some train trips provide lectures, sightseeing stops, and special activities like the Mystery Express.

Paragraph C: Ecotourism is popular with people who are interested in nature. They can explore the wildlife and environment on their trips.

Paragraph D: People can study or do volunteer work as they travel. They can help others and learn at the same time.

Paragraph E: Travel can be cheap. With courier travel, a person carries some materials for a company in return for a discount on the airfare. Traveling by a freighter is also cheaper than on a cruise ship.

Paragraph F: Soon there may be trip into outerspace. Some people already travel high into the atmosphere to experience zero-gravity, but it's very expensive.

Discussing the Reading

5 Small Group Discussion. Page 123.
Arrange students in groups of four to answer the questions. Allow about 15-20 minutes for the group discussions. When all groups are finished, invite volunteers to share the most interesting responses and ideas from their groups.

Answers will vary.

Part 3 Building Vocabulary and Study Skills

1 Expressions and Idioms. Page 123.
Read the expressions and idioms aloud. You may want to have students look back in the reading selections in Part 1 and Part 2 for the expressions. Encourage volunteers to explain the meanings of ones they remember or to use them in sentences. Then have students complete the exercise. Go over the answers with the class. Ask volunteers to create sentences for the expressions that were not used.

Answers: 1. hold back   2. get around
3. private eye   4. track down   5. in the market for   6. rough it   7. goes without saying   8. out of this world

2 Participles as Adjectives. Page 124.
After you read the explanation and instructions together, call attention to the example. Then have students complete the exercise individually, using a dictionary as needed. Go over the answers together.

Answers: 1. interested, thrilling (challenging, relaxing)   2. challenging (tiring), tired, relaxing, relaxed   3. exciting (thrilling, challenging), excited (interested), terrified (horrified), frightening (horrifying, terrifying)   4. interesting, addicted, thrilled, terrified (horrified)

3 Increasing Reading Speed. Page 124.
Read the instructions aloud before having students complete the exercise.

Answers:
break up 2; out of this world 2; pulled into 2; in a hurry 3; private eye 3

by train 3; take your turn 2; see the sights 2; in the market 2; get around 2

open trade 2; on your own 2 sign up for 2; above board 3; hold back 1

global crime 1; point out 3; take place 2; social order 2; child care 3

Part 4 Reading in the Real World

1 Reading Difficult Material. Page 126.
Read the suggestions together. Call attention to the questions below for students to think about before reading the following selection. Clarify vocabulary in the questions as needed. You may want to have students discuss the questions in small groups. Ask volunteers from each group to report their responses. Guide students to summarize the responses.

2 Scanning for Information. Page 126.
Point out the chart on page 127. Then read the instructions together. Remind students to look for

the specific information for the chart as they are reading. Have students complete the chart individually and compare their charts in small groups. Go over the answers with the whole class.

Sample Answers:
Characteristics of High-Crime Cultures

Culture: multicultural, industrialized, democratic, economic choice, individualism

Parenting: not required knowledge, skills, or income to be parents; no support system for parents, parents solely responsible for care of the children

Wealth: large difference between rich and poor

Social Order: no clear difference between right and wrong; social order is broken down; old rules and ideas are abandoned; no bond with others

Characteristics of Low-Crime Cultures

Culture: isolated, homogeneous culture, similar ethnic groups, similar income levels and values, traditional of discipline

Parenting: all citizens responsible for children; parents receive support and preparation

Wealth: equally shared

Social Order: traditional social order; authoritative society; close bond with others

3 **Discussion. Page 129.**

Allow students to discuss their personal responses to the questions and reading selection. Have volunteers report their ideas and views on society and crime.

Talk It Over

Applying the Death Penalty

Allow students to discuss their opinions in small groups. Alternatively, you may want to have students write the answer to this question. Encourage them to support their opinions with examples or other supporting details.

Culture Note

This is a sensitive and controversial topic. Be aware of traditional values and beliefs of students in the class as you decide whether to use the Talk It Over exercise or not.

Video Activities: Teen Talk

Before You Watch

Read the questions aloud and ask students to discuss their answers in small groups. Have students report to the class their answers.

Answers will vary.

Watch [on video]

Ask students to read the questions before they view the video. Then play the video and have students circle their answers.

Answers: 1. b 2. a, d

Watch Again [on video]

Ask students to read the statements. Then, replay the video and have students complete their responses. Go over the answers with the whole class.

Answers: 1. Drugs, depression, overloaded with work 2. Talking 3. Resources (for problem solving and crises.

After You Watch

Bring in some sample advice columns for students to look at. You may want to have students use specific letter or find other letters. Then have students respond to them. Ask volunteers to share their letters and responses.

Answers will vary.

Language and Communication

Goals

- **Read about and discuss animal communication**
- **Understand main idea**
- **Get meaning from context and logic**
- **Categorize**
- **Understand punctuation**
- **Understand outlines**
- **Skim for main ideas**
- **Make inferences**
- **Distinguish fact from theory**
- **Summarize**
- **Categorize**
- **Understand prefixes and suffixes**
- **Recognize word roots**
- **Scan for information**
- **Answer comprehension questions: stated and implied**

Part 1 If We Could Talk With the Animals...

Before You Read

1 Getting Started. Page 132.
Have volunteers describe the animals in the pictures on page 132. Then ask students to discuss the questions in small groups. Have volunteers report their groups' answers.

Sample Answers:
1. The animals might communicate with sounds, touching each other, body language/signals, facial expressions, bubbles.

2. Whales might need some vocal organs and hearing organs to communicate.

3. Communication is sending and receiving a message (verbal, visual, etc.). Language is a complex system of expressing ideas and messages with words, phrases, and sentences.

4. I think animals can learn to respond to language, but I don't think they can learn the grammar and rules for manipulating a language.

2 Vocabulary Preview. Page 133.
Read the words aloud as students check the ones they don't know. Remind them to look back at this list later after completing the reading selection exercises to check their understand of the new words.

Read

3 If We Could Talk With the Animals... Page 133. [on tape/CD]
Call attention to the guiding question in the instructions. Explain that students should think about this as they read. Play the tape or CD and have students follow along in their books. If needed, stop the recording occasionally to check understanding and to point out vocabulary words. Then, listen and read a second time.

After You Read

4 Getting the Main Ideas. Page 137.
After students complete the exercise, discuss the answers. Ask volunteers to correct the false statements to make them true and to explain why some of the statements are impossible to know.

Answers: 1. T 2. F 3. F 4. T 5. F 6. I 7. F

5 Getting Meaning from Context. Page 137.
Go over the instructions. Call attention to the key expressions and punctuation clues for definitions within a text. Then have students complete the exercise. Check the answers together.

Answers: 2. trail 3. upright 4. swagger 5. echolocation 6. pod 7. gender 8. syntax

6 Page 138.
Have students complete the exercise individually. Then go over the possible answers. You may want to have students think of other items that belong in these categories.

Answers: 1. creatures 2. primates

7 Page 138.
After students complete the exercise, invite volunteers to share their responses. Discuss any different responses.

Answers: 1. head back ("home") 2. wagging 3. reassure 4. prey

8 Page 138.
Students can work individually to find the words. Go over the answers together.

Answers: 1. grin 2. vocalize

9 Page 138.
Read the instructions together and point out the example. Remind students that some words have more than one meaning. Then have students complete the exercise. Go over the answers together. Ask volunteers to suggest sentences that use the words with their different meanings.

Answers: 1. feeds 2. head 3. organs 4. subject 5. pick up 6. coin

10 Understanding Punctuation. Page 139.
Go over the uses of italics and quotation marks. Ask students to find examples of each in the reading selection. Then have students mark other examples and decide on the reason for their uses. Go over the answers with the class.

Answers:
Paragraph B: *The "Language" of Smell* (italics: title; quotation marks: word means something different)
"smell-messages" (word means something different)
"home" (word means something different)
Paragraph C: *Body Language* (title)
"dance" (word means something different)
"saying" (word means something different)
"I want to play." (direct speech)
"smiles" (word means something different)
Paragraph D: *Vocalizations* (title)
"songs" (word means something different)
Paragraph E: "talking" (word means something different)
"There's a tall blue human coming from the north." (direct speech)
very (emphasis)
Paragraph F: *Symbols* (title)
Ball, basket, pipe (the word...)
Big, small, red (the word...)
Left, right (the word...)
Go, take (the word...)
In, under (the word...)
"Go to the ball on your right and take it to the basket." (direct speech)
Paragraph G: *Primate Studies* (title)
Paragraph H: "take the potato outdoors" (direct speech)
"go outdoors and get the potato" (direct speech)
"You me out" (direct speech)
"Me banana you banana me you give." (direct speech)
"water bird" (the word...)
"green banana" (the word...)
"Me sad." (direct speech)
Paragraph I: *Language?* (title)

"Lana tomorrow scare snake river monster" (direct speech)

planum temporale (foreign language)

Science (title)

"essentially identical" (direct speech)

do (emphasis)

Paragraph J: *Conclusions* (title)

"Is it language?" (direct speech)

syntax (the word ...)

"Some people think of language.... or you don't." (direct speech)

"a continuum of skills" (direct speech)

11 Checking Your Understanding. Page 139.

Students can complete the exercise individually. When they are finished, have them check their answers with others in the class. Review possible answers.

Sample Answer:

Animals communicate in various ways: smells, body language, and sounds. Some animals can also learn to communicate using symbols. Animals seem to be able to understand language, but they are not able to use language to communicate beyond a very basic level.

12 Understanding Outlines. Page 139.

Review the organization and format of an outline. Point out the general topics and specific topics in the exercise. Then have students fill in the missing topics, looking back at the reading selection as needed. Go over possible responses.

Sample Answers:

II. A. 2. Send a warning.
3. Mark territories
4. Where food is located
B. 2. Ant
III. Body language
B. Dog
1. Happiness
2. Want to play
C. Chimpanzees
1. Walking and waving arms = angry
2. Low to ground = afraid, nervous
3. Smile = nervous grin
4. Hugs, kisses, touches = reassurance
IV. A. Whales
2. Songs = to communicate with group
B. 1. Alert to danger
2. a. tell shape, size, color
b. tell gender (male or female), dog or coyote
c. degree of danger
A. Hand signals
1. Ball, basket, pipe
2. Adjectives: big, small, red
3. Directions: right, left
4. Verbs: go, take
5. Prepositions: in, under
B. 2. Understand subjects and objects
3. Follow new commands using known vocabulary
VI. A. 2. Kanzi—lexigrams, keyboard and symbols
B. 2. Combine words into short sentences
3. Coin new words and phrases
4. Express emotion
VII. A. 1. Only vocabulary level of 2½ year old
2. Gap between language ability of humans and chimps
B. 2. 99% in chimps is the same as in humans

Discussing the Reading

13 Small Group Discussion. Page 142.
Arrange students in groups of five or six to answer the questions about pets and animal communication. Ask a volunteer from each group to share the most interesting items from their groups discussions.

Answers will vary.

Part 2 "Parentese"

Before You Read

1 Preparing to Read. Page 142.
Read the questions aloud, explaining vocabulary as needed. Have students discuss their answers to the questions with a partner or in small groups. Ask volunteers to share their ideas and responses with the class.

Answers will vary.

**2 Skimming for Main Ideas. Page 143.
[on tape/CD]**
You may want to assign this exercise for homework or to have students work individually on it in class. Go over the answers with the class, asking volunteers to justify their choices of main idea.

Answers: A. 5 B. 3 C. 1 D. 1 E. 4

After You Read

3 Getting Meaning from Context. Page 145.
Remind students to use context clues and logic to find the specific words. Students can complete the exercise individually or in pairs. Go over the answers together. Ask volunteers to use the words in their own sentences.

Answers: 1. verbal 2. glue 3. emotions
4. realize 5. respond 6. apparently
7. nature 8. nurture 9. evidence

4 Making Inferences. Page 146.
Review making inferences. Then have students complete the exercise individually or for homework. Remind students to look back at the reading selection to find the appropriate information. Go over the answers with the group.

Answers:
Paragraph A: 1. √ ... women are more verbal.... But she says this is a stereotype. 2. √ ...women are more verbal... in private situations ... but ... mean talk more in public situations....

Paragraph B: 3. — 4. √ There is also fare more talk about emotions, especially sadness...

Paragraph C: 5. √ ... are a little less developed... They don't vocalize... have as much eye contact.... 6. —

Paragraph D: 7. √ The situation or context influences the conversation. 8. —

Paragraph E: 9. — 10. —

5 Distinguishing Facts from Theories. Page 147.
Read the explanation and instructions together. Clarify the difference between facts and theories. Call attention to the sample words and expressions associated with facts and theories. Have students complete the exercise, referring to the reading selection to find the exact wording. Go over the answers together.

Answers: 1. Theory 2. Fact 3. Fact
4. Fact 5. Theory 6. Theory

6 Summarizing. Page 148.
You may want to assign specific paragraphs for pairs of students to summarize. Later, have students who wrote summaries of the same paragraphs compare their summaries in small

groups. Tell them to check for overall agreement of main idea and important details.

Sample Answers:

Paragraph A: Men and women have different styles of speaking. Men speak more in public situations, but women speak more in private situations. These behaviors begin in childhood.

Paragraph B: Parents talk differently to their sons and daughters. They use more language with the girls, giving more details and talking more about emotions.

Paragraph C: Parents may talk more to baby girls because they are a little more developed than the boys. They have more eye contact and vocalize more.

Paragraph D: The toys that children play with also may affect language ability. Cars and typical toys for boys involve more doing things. Dolls and toy grocery stores, which are typical toys for girls, involve more conversation.

Paragraph E: Parents should try to give a variety of toys to children: task-oriented toys like cars and social-oriented toys like grocery store. Then children will practice conversations for all types of situations.

Discussing the Reading

7 Small Group Discussion. Page 148.

Arrange students in groups of four to answers to the questions. Allow 15-20 minutes for the group discussions. Invite volunteers to share the most interesting responses and ideas from their groups.

Answers will vary.

Talk It Over

Have students discuss their responses in groups or to prepare written responses to the questions about their own experiences.

Beyond the Text

Ask students to share their findings with the class and to give their own personal reactions to the current popular toys.

Part 3 Building Vocabulary and Study Skills

1 Categorizing. Page 148.

Remind students that categories are general headings or divisions. After students have compared answers with a partner, go over the exercise. Ask volunteers for other items that might be included in the categories.

Sample Answers: 1. physical contact 2. emotions (feelings) 3. scientists 4. verbal communication 5. animals (mammals) 6. ocean mammals 7. insects 8. expressions for theories 9. expressions for facts 10. verbs that show a cause and effect relationship

2 Prefixes and Suffixes. Page 149.

Call attention to the list of affixes and meanings. You may want to have volunteers suggest words with these prefixes and suffixes. Then read the instructions and have students complete the exercise individually. Go over the answers together.

Answers: 1. conversation, converse, conversational; 2. n., adj., n.; linguistics, linguists, linguistic; 3. n., v., adv.; reassure, reassurance, reassuringly; 4. adj., n., adv.; ability, able, ably; 5. v., adj., adv.; Apparently, apparent, appear; 6. adj., v., adj.; simplify, simplified, simple; 7. adj., v., n.; vocalize, vocal, vocalization

3 Word Roots. Page 151.

Read the instructions aloud before having students complete the exercise. As you go over the answers, have volunteers suggest other words that contain these roots. Then have students prepare their own sentences (similar to those in Exercise 2) for the words in the chart. Students can exchange sentences for additional practice using the words.

Answers:
definition, define, definite, definitely
presentation, present, presentable, presently
nature, naturalize, natural, naturally
existence, exist, existent
psychology, psychological, psychologically
prediction, predict, predictable, predictably

4 Learning New Vocabulary. Page 152.
As you read the explanations and instructions together, allow students to share other ideas they have for learning new vocabulary. Encourage students to complete their own vocabulary log following the suggestions in the activity. Suggest that they add other words related to specific academic classes or subject areas of interest to them. Occasionally, ask volunteers to share some interesting words that they have included in their vocabulary logs.

Part 4 Reading in the Real World

1 Preparing to Read. Page 153.
Have students discuss the questions in groups. Ask volunteers from each group to present the groups' ideas. Guide students to summarize the responses and to make predications about the topic of the next reading.

Answers will vary.

2 Vocabulary Preview. Page 153.
Call attention to the heads/categories of the vocabulary words. You may want to read the words aloud. If students are familiar with any of the words, encourage them to tell where they have seen the words before and/or what they

mean. Remind students to use this glossary as they read the article

Focus on Testing

Comprehension Questions on Reading Tests
Read the testing tips together. Review the meanings of "stated" and "implied." Then have students go on to Exercise 3.

3 Scanning for Information. Page 154.
Remind students to look over the questions in Exercise 4 before reading the article. This will guide their reading and help them mark the important details. Have them read and answer the questions. Go over the answers with the group.

4 Checking Your Understanding. Page 157.
Students can look back at the reading and their markings as they answer the questions. As you go over the answers with the group, have volunteers point out specific passages in the reading that support their responses.

Answers: 1. a 2. e 3. d 4. c 5. c 6. d 7. c 8. c 9. c

Beyond the Text

You may want to have student complete one of the interview projects. Depending on the group, go over possible questions to use in the interview. Have students report their findings to the class.

Video Activities: Technology for the Disabled

Before You Watch
Read the questions aloud and ask students to discuss their answers in small groups. Have students report to the class their answers.

Sample Answers:
1. Problems that have limited or reduced a person's ability to do things.
2. Paraplegic: a person whose lower part of the body is paralyzed usually because of a spinal cord injury. Quadriplegic: a person who is paralyzed from the neck down.
3. Some difficulties encountered by disabled people are: using transportation, using stairs, moving around, etc.

Watch [on video]
Ask students to read the questions before they view the video. Then play the video and have students discuss the answers.

Answers:
1. The technology reads the pages for him.
2. He uses a special infrared device in his glasses which acts as the cursors on the computer screen. He has a special fiber switch on his cheek for sending signals.
3. About 10% of Americans have a disability.

Watch Again [on video]
Ask students to read the statements. Then, replay the video and have students complete their responses. Go over the answers with the whole class.

Answers: 1. blind, disability 2. head, eye

After You Watch
Assign or have students select people from the list for a research project. Invite volunteers to present their findings to the class or post the written biographies on a bulletin board for others in the class to read.

Tastes and Preferences

Goals

- **Read about and discuss art history**
- **Understand main idea**
- **Get meaning from context**
- **Understand outlines**
- **Recognize connecting and summarizing words**
- **Make inferences**
- **Skim for main idea**
- **Summarize**
- **Discuss art and beauty**
- **Understand words with similar meanings**
- **Recognize connotations**
- **Increase reading speed**
- **Identify words with opposite meanings**
- **Use analogies**
- **Scan for information**
- **Distinguish fact from theory**

Part 1 What Can We Learn from Art?

Before You Read

1 Getting Started. Page 162.
Have volunteers describe the artwork in the pictures on pages 162-163. Then allow students to discuss the questions in small groups. After 10-15 minutes, have volunteers report their groups' answers.

Sample Answers:
1. They are photos of important artwork from different cultures and different historical periods. The art is probably in museums.

2. The first photo is a cave painting of large animals. It's on a piece of rock. The people who made it were probably cave people from prehistoric times. The animals are ones they hunted.

   The second photo is of an oil painting by a Spanish painter. The painting shows army soldiers shooting some citizens.

   The third photo is modern art mural by Picasso. It shows the horrors of war (based on what happened in the town of Guernica).

   The fourth photo is art that is on the masks or headdresses of some African tribespeople in Mali. The figures show animals found in the local area.

   The fifth is from the Pacific islands. It looks like a figure of a god or spirit.

   The last is a intricately decorated bowl with some Arabic writing around it.

3. The photos all show things or events that are/were important to the particular people. They are different in terms of materials used, style, and purpose.

4. Answers will vary.

2 Vocabulary Preview. Page 163.
Read the words aloud as students check the ones they don't know. Remind them to look back at this list later after completing the reading selection exercises to check their understand of the new words.

Read

3 What Can We Learn from Art? Page 163. [on tape/CD]
Have students find the headings in the reading selection and make predictions about it. Call attention to the guiding question in the instructions. Explain that students should think

about this as they read. Play the tape or CD and have students follow along in their books. If needed, stop the recording occasionally to check understanding and to point out vocabulary words. Then, listen a second time.

After You Read

4 Getting the Main Ideas. Page 166.

Read the instructions together and have students complete the exercise. Discuss the answers together.

Answers: 1. P 2. W 3. T 4. T 5. CH
6. T 7. I 8. I 9. T

5 Getting Meaning from Context. Page 167.

Go over the instructions. Students can complete the exercise individually or in pairs. As a group, go over the answers.

Answers:

1. painting; verb, artist, showed or pictured

2. history books, information, facts; emotions and opinions; adjective, history books, opinions, factual or true, adjective, emotions and opinions, objective

3. palaces, buildings; noun, building, Islamic, Islamic religious buildings

Point out the example below and have students identify clues in the sentences that can be used to guess the meaning of *images*.

6 Writing Definitions. Page 168.

Have students complete the exercise individually. Then, go over the possible answers. In addition, you may want to have students use the words in sentences.

Answers:

1. Islamic belief, religious, new religion, stopped using them; sacred or important to a religious group

2. beauty, attractive; something that adds beauty

3. startling beauty, great beauty; very beautiful

7 Identifying Words and Expressions. Page 168.

After students complete the exercise, invite volunteers to give the answers and use the words in sentences.

Answers: 1. essential 2. caves 3. cliffs
4. spelunkers 5. come upon 6. crawling
7. tunnels 8. archeologists 9. worship
10. misuse 11. absence 12. arabesques
13. calligraphy 14. significant 15. spear
16. target 17. destination 18. headdresses
19. functional 20. foretell 21. admire

8 Understanding Outlines. Page 169.

Review the organization and format of an outline as you read the instructions and explanation together. Have students refer back to the reading as they fill in the subtopics on the outline on page 170. Students can compare their completed outlines. Go over the answers as needed.

Answers:

II.   A. Prehistoric, Stone Age
        B. Purpose—a mystery; possibilities
            1. Assurance of success in hunting
            2. Worship animal "god"
III.   B. Picasso's Guernica
        C. Mexican social art
IV.   A. Christian images in church
        B. Islamic designs and Arabic calligraphy
V.   A. Art serving a practical function
        B. 1. People of Solomon Islands (figures on spears and boats to guide them)
            2. Bakongo people (headdresses to help crops grow)
            3. Bakongo people (statues for predictions and protection)
VI.   A. Decoration
        B. Function
VII.   A. Tribal people moving to urban areas
        B. The influence of traditional art on Picasso and Gauguin
        C. The effect of Japanese painting

9 Connecting and Summarizing. Page 171.

Point out the words and expressions that indicate a summary of material. Then have students look back at the reading selection for these expressions. Students can complete the exercise individually. Go over the answers together.

Answers:
1. In short, art expresses the essential qualities of a time and a place, and a study of it clearly offers us a deeper understanding than can be found in most history books.
2. In summary, a personal and emotional view of history can be presented through art.
3. Thus, on palaces, mosques, and other buildings, Islamic artists have created exquisite arabesques—decorations of great beauty with images of flowers and geometric forms (for example, circles, squares, and triangles).
4. To sum up, art in many cultures is believed to serve essential, practical functions.
5. As we've seen, art depends on culture.
6. In brief, the way in which people enjoy art depends on their culture.
7. In conclusion, art is a reflection of various cultures.
8. The result is that as the world gets "smaller," the art of each culture becomes more international

Main Idea: 1

10 Checking Your Understanding. Page 171.

Ask students to answer the question on page 163. You may want to have students share their answer with partners or in small groups. Have volunteers share their answers with the class. Point out the important information that is common in all the answers.

Sample Answer:
From art history, you can learn about a culture. It gives information about the religion, beliefs, and feelings of the people. Since people used art to decorate practical items, you can learn about their daily life. People use art to express their view about politics. They use it to show their faith and belief. The history of art shows

how people and cultures have changed through time.

11 Making Inferences. Page 172.

Have students complete the exercise. Point out that more than one answer is possible. Students may want to look back at the reading selection as they work. Go over the possible responses.

Answers: 1. c 2. a, b, c 3. a, c
4. b, c, d

Discussing the Reading

12 Small Group Discussion. Page 172.

Arrange students in groups of five or six to answer the questions about art in their native cultures. Ask a volunteer from each group to share the most interesting items from their groups discussions.

Answers will vary.

Part 2 Fashion: The Art of the Body

1 Skimming for Main Ideas. Page 173. [on tape/CD]

Read and discuss the explanation and example of an implied main idea. Guide students to notice the details that contribute to the main idea. Point out the instructions for the exercise. Then have students read the paragraphs and answer the questions. You may play the tape or CD as students follow along in their books. Go over the questions as a group or have students compare their answers in pairs.

Answers:
A: 1. b 2. a, c, d 3. c
B: 1. d 2. b, d 3. b
C: 1. d 2. b, c 3. a
D: 1. c 2. b, c, d 3. b
E: 1. a 2. a, b, c 3. c

After You Read

2 Making Inferences. Page 178.

You may want to assign this exercise for homework or to have students work in pairs on it in class. Go over the answers with the class, asking volunteers to justify their choices of main idea.

Answers:

1. —
2. wear animal fur to protect them against the cold winter weather; wear long, loose clothing for protection against the sun
3. —
4. These days, in most societies (especially in the West), rank or status is exhibited through regulation of dress on in the military... the divisions between different classes are becoming less clear...
5. —
6. In modern societies, though, cosmetics are used mostly by women, who often feel naked, unclothed, without makeup when in public...
7. —
8. ....like a tribal hunter without his warpaint...

3 Summarizing. Page 179.

You may want to assign specific paragraphs for students to summarize. Later, have students who wrote summaries of the same paragraphs compare their summaries in small groups. Tell them to check for overall agreement of main idea and important details.

Sample Answers:

A: In many societies, there used to be strict laws describing how different classes of people could dress. Today, the divisions between classes are not so strict so people often wear similar clothing.

B: Tattooing and scarification are two traditional types of body decorations. Tattoos are designs made with dyes under the skin. Scarification is dirt or ashes put into cuts. Tattooing is popular now among young people.

C: There are different ideas about how people should look. In some societies, women should be fat. In others, they should be slim. Some societies prefer dark hair or skin and in others they prefer light hair and skin.

D: Each society defines "attractive" differently. To some, teeth should be white and straight. In others, they should be black and pointed. Some societies like large rings in the lips of people. Others don't.

E: In some tribal societies, men wore facial paint. In many modern societies, women wear make-up or facial paint. They feel they are more attractive with it.

Discussing the Reading

4 Small Group Discussion. Page 179.

Arrange students in groups of four to answers to the questions. Allow about 15-20 minutes for the group discussions. When all groups are finished, invite volunteers to share the most interesting responses and ideas from their groups.

Answers will vary.

Talk It Over

Art and Beauty

Depending on the class, you may want to have students discuss their interpretations and responses to the quotations in groups. Encourage them to share quotes or proverbs related to art and beauty that they know.

Sample Answers:

- There is beauty in simplicity. Too much of something is not beautiful.
- Beauty means different things to different people.
- As people get older, they lose the youthful natural beauty and their image and appearance are the result of how they live and feel.
- Beautiful things are nice to look at, but they are often impractical and useless.

- It is more important to have something that works than something that looks great but cannot be used.
- Beautiful art is universal. The people that create great art are recognized around the world in all societies and cultures.

Beyond the Text

Ask students to share their findings with the class and to give their own personal reactions to the beauty ads and treatments.

Part 3 Building Vocabulary and Study Skills

1 Words with Similar Meanings. Page 181.

Call attention to the examples of words with similar meanings. Clarify the slight differences in their definitions. Point out that the words cannot be substituted for each other in many cases. Have students work in pairs to complete the exercise. Remind them to check in a dictionary if they cannot decide. Go over the answers and ask volunteers to use the words in different sentences to highlight their different meanings.

Answers:
1. b 2. a 3. c
4. c 5. a 6. b
7. a 8. b 9. c
10. c 11. a 12. b
13. b 14. a 15. c

2 Word Meanings. Page 182.

Read the instructions and example together. Point out the one word that has a more general meaning than the others. Have students complete the exercise. As you go over the answers, have volunteers explain the general meaning of the one word and tell how it includes the other words.

Answers: 2. artist 3. entertainer
4. traveler 5. transportation 6. royalty
7. religion 8. crime

3 Connotations of Words. Page 182.

Read the instructions and examples aloud. Point out that the words may have similar meanings, but the words evoke different feelings that are negative or positive. Call attention to the dictionary entries and ask students to find samples of information about the connotation of the words. Then have students complete the exercise individually. Go over the answers together. Encourage students to suggest situations or sentences where the words with positive and negative connotations might be used appropriately.

Answers: 1. + 2. – 3. – 4. + 5. –
6. +

4 Words with Polite Connotations. Page 183.

Have students refer back to the dictionary entries as they complete the exercise. Go over the answers with the group.

Answers: 1. slim 3. plump 4. matronly
6. heavy

5 Words with Strong Meanings. Page 183.

Students should look back at the dictionary entries as needed for this exercise. Review the answers with the group.

Answers: 1. beautiful 2. hideous
3. beautiful 4. ugly 5. beautiful 6. ugly

6 Appropriate Words. Page 183.

Point out that there is more than one correct answer for each of the items. Ask volunteers to justify their choices as you go over the answers.

Answers: 1. b, c, d 2. a, c 3. c, d

7 Words with Similar Meanings. Page 183.

Students can work in groups to prepare lists of similar words. Ask volunteers from each group to share their words. Make a chart on the board for words with positive connotations and words with negative connotations. Discuss situations when the different words might be heard or used.

8 Increasing Reading Speed. Page 184.
Read the instructions aloud before having students complete the exercise. Point out that in this exercise they are looking for words with similar meanings, not the exact same word.

Answers:

test, area, instance, school, enjoyable

statue, plants, move, foretell, fight

opportunity, wealthy, different, pollution, therapist

shape, design, depict, bargain, strength

9 Finding Words with Opposite Meanings. Page 185.
Before students complete the exercises, remind them that they are looking for words with opposite meanings.

Answers:

terrible, villages, individual, unusual, specifically

traditional, death, emotional, victim, public

useless, young, lose, improve, different

Focus on Testing

Using Analogies
Read the information on analogy activities together. Call attention to the examples of common relationships used in analogies. Ask volunteers for other sets of words that might show these relationships. Point out that other relationships might be possible, such as antonyms (opposites), part to whole, tool with its use, etc. Give examples as needed. Then have students complete the exercise. Allow students to compare answers and talk about the relationships. Then go over the answers with the whole class.

Sample Answers: 1. expensive (opposites/antonyms) 2. hunter (the hunted and the hunter) 3. compulsion (adjective to noun) 4. student (boss to worker) 5. rural (noun to adjective) 6. small (synonym) 7. radioactive gas (example to general category) 8. North America (country to continent) 9. economy (profession to subject of study) 10. smile (synonym)

Part 4 Reading in the Real World

1 Scanning for Information. Page 187.
Have students preview the article, noting the title, pictures, and captions. You may want to have students predict what the article will be about. Then read the instructions aloud. After students read through the questions in Exercise 2, have them read the article and complete exercise 2.

2 Checking Your Understanding. Page 189.
Go over the answers after students have completed the exercise individually. You may want to have students find the phrases and sentences in the article where the answers are found.

Answers: 1. e 2. b 3. e 4. c 5. e 6. d 7. e

3 Distinguishing Fact from Theory. Page 191.
Review the meanings of "fact" and "theory." Ask volunteers for commonly used words and expressions for theories that were presented in Chapter 7. Then have students complete the exercise. As you go over the answers, have volunteers explain why the statements are facts or theories.

Answers: 1. Fact 2. Theory 3. Fact 4. Theory 5. Theory

Video Activities: The Coffee Lover

Before You Watch
Read the questions aloud and ask students to discuss their answers in small groups. Have students report their answers to the class.

Answers will vary.

Watch [on video]
Ask students to read the questions. Play the video and have students discuss the answers. You may want to ask students their personal reactions to the number of cups of coffee that Kat drinks and her views about coffee.

Answers: 1. 10-14 2. No

Watch Again [on video]
Ask students to read the statements. Then, replay the video and have students complete the exercise. Go over the answers with the whole class.

Answers: 1. T 2. T 3. F 4. T 5. F

After You Watch
Have students research coffee using dictionaries, encyclopedias, the Internet, or other reference materials. Ask volunteers to present their findings to the class.

Answers:
1. The word "coffee" can be traced from Italian, Turkish, and Arabic.
2. • The coffee plant is an evergreen tree. It produces a berry with a seed which is dried and then roasted. The plants grow about 20 feet tall. They grow in subtropical regions.
   • The plant is believed to have originated in Northern Africa (Ethiopia) and was transported to the Arabian peninsula (Yemen).

- It was first used as a drink in Turkey where the beans were roasted, crushed, and boiled in water.
- Coffee came to North America in the early 1700's when a French captain brought a plant across the Atlantic to Martinique. From there, the plants were spread throughout the subtropical regions of Central and South America.
- There are two main species of coffee: *coffea arabica* and *coffea robusta*. Since the soil, altitude, weather, cultivation, etc. influence the quality of the coffee beans, each country or region produces coffee beans with unique characteristics.

New Frontiers

Goals
- **Read a diagram**
- **Preview a reading selection**
- **Read about and discuss the brain**
- **Understand main idea**
- **Get meaning from context**
- **Distinguish fact from theory**
- **Skim for main idea**
- **Make inferences**
- **Understand words with similar meanings**
- **Recognize categories**
- **Use word roots and affixes to guess meanings**
- **Summarize a passage**

Part 1 The Human Brain— New Discoveries

Before You Read

1 Getting Started. Page 194.
Call attention to the diagram of the brain. Point out the parts of the brain and have students identify the functions. Then have students discuss the questions in small groups. After 10-15 minutes, have volunteers report their groups' answers.

Sample Answers:
1. The cerebrum and cortex, frontal lobe, and temporal lobe might be used by a person composing music. To throw a ball, a person might use the cerebellum, cerebrum and cortex, and parietal lobe. To paint a picture, a person might use the

occipital lobe, parietal lobe, cerebrum and cortex, and cerebellum.
2. The active areas of the brain would be in the neocortex (cerebrum and cortex, the thalamus, and the hypothalamus).
3. Answers will vary.
4. I think the men in photo B might be in better health, because they seem more active and they are interacting with each other.

2 Preparing to Read. Page 195.
Read the suggestions aloud for surveying a reading selection. Call attention to subheadings in the reading selection as needed. Then have students complete the exercise. As you go over the answers, have volunteers predict what information they might find under the different subheadings.

Answers:
Parts of Brain
Left Brain/Right Brain: Creativity
Memory—True or False?
The Teen Brain
Difference in Male and Female Brains
Wired for Music?
The Mystery of the Mind-Body Relationship

3 Page 196.
Remind students to look back at the diagram and photos on pages 194-195 as they complete the exercise. Go over the answers and have volunteers explain what information they used to determine their answers.

Answers: 1. √ 2. — 3. √ 4. √ 5. — 6. — 7. √ 8. — 9. √ 10. √ 11. √

4 Vocabulary Preview. Page 196.
Read the words aloud as students check the ones they don't know. Remind them to check their understand of the new words after completing the reading selection exercises.

5 The Human Brain—New Discoveries. Page 197. [on tape/CD]

Play the tape or CD and have students follow along in their books. Pause the recording occasionally to check understanding and to point out vocabulary words. Then, listen a second time.

After You Read

7 Getting the Main Ideas. Page 199.

Read the instructions together and have students complete the exercise. Discuss the answers together.

Answers: 1. T 2. T/I 3. I 4. F 5. F
6. F 7. T

Focus on Testing

Getting Meaning from Context

Read the tips aloud about standardized exams. Remind students of different types of context clues that are useful, such as: definitions, explanations, examples, comparisons, and contrasts. Then have students complete the exercise, referring back to the reading selection for the complete contexts. As you go over the answers, have volunteers point out the clues they used to make their answers.

Answers: 1. d 2. b 3. c 4. d 5. c
6. a 7. d 8. c

7 Distinguishing Facts from Theories. Page 201.

Review the difference between fact and theory. As you read the information in Exercise 7, call attention to the words and expressions that usually indicate facts and theories. Ask volunteers to find examples of some of the words and expressions in the reading selection on pages 197-199.

8 Fact or Theory? Page 201.

After students complete the exercise, go over the answers. Ask volunteers to read the passages in the selection that support their responses.

Answers: 1. Fact 2. Theory 3. Theory
4. Theory 5. Fact 6. Theory 7. Fact
8. Fact 9. Theory 10. Fact 11. Theory
12. Fact 13. Theory 14. Fact 15. Fact
16. Theory 17. Theory

9 Checking Your Understanding. Page 202.

Have students refer back to the reading as they answer the questions from Exercise 3. Students can compare their answers with classmates before you go over the answers with the entire class.

Sample Answers:

1. The subcortex controls basic functions: breathing, eating, drinking, and sleeping. The cerebellum helps motor functions and balance. The neocortex is the control center for thinking. The cerebrum controls active thought. The left hemisphere controls the right side of the body and logical thinking. The right hemisphere controls the left side of the body and emotional, creative, and artistic functions. The corpus callosum connects the two hemispheres.

2. Human brains are different from animal brains in that animals do not have the neocortex.

3. Some people are more creative than others because they exercise the right side of the brain more.

4. The left side of the brain is used for logical thought and is exercised in school with reading, writing, and mathematics. The right side of the brain is used in dreams, and insights, and creative activities.

5. —

6. It is possible to have a memory of something that never happened; these are false memories. Different parts of the brain store different parts of memories, so when the middle of the brain pulls all the memories together, the memories may not be of true events.

7. —

8. Teenagers' brains are different from adults' brains. The brain (corpus callosum) is still growing during the teen years. Since it is involved in self-awareness and intelligence, teens are still developing in these areas.

9. —

10. The brain influences a person's musical ability. Research has shown that the corpus callosum is larger in musicians than in non-musicians.

11. The brain can cause people to get sick or become well. Positive thinking helps people get better sooner than negative thinking.

Part 2 Personality—Nature or Nurture?

1 Skimming for Main Ideas. Page 202. [on tape/CD]

Read the instructions for the exercise together. Then have students read the paragraphs and answer the questions. Point out that more than one answer may be correct. You may play the tape or CD as students follow along in their books. Go over the questions as a group or have students compare their answers in pairs.

Sample Answers:

B—1. c 2. b, c, e 3. ...twins that grow up separately indicate that genetics is important in determining characteristics, interests, and personality.

C—1. e 2. b, c, 3. ...many behavioral characteristics (such as: optimism, pessimism, happiness, thrill-seeking) are influenced by genes.

D—1. b 2. a, c, d, e 3. ...the combination of genes affects a person's personality.

E—1. b 2. a, b, d, e 3. ... people should choose the best environment to fit with their talents and personality traits.

After You Read

2 Making Inferences. Page 206.

You may want to assign this exercise for homework or to have students work in pairs on it in class. Go over the answers with the class, asking volunteers to justify their choices of main idea.

Answers:

1. √ ... is not a new one.... Go back at least several hundred years.
2. —
3. √ ...the degree to which a trait is due to genes ("nature") instead of environment...
4. √ ... it is 80% heritable....
5. —
6. √ Instead, many genes work together...
7. —

Talk It Over

Genes for Crime?

Depending on the class, you may want to have students choose a side in this question and have a debate. Encourage students to give examples or reasons for their views.

Beyond the Text

If students are interested, have them look for recent discoveries and studies related to genetics. Encourage students to share their findings with the class and to give their own personal reactions to the findings and tests.

Part 3 Building Vocabulary and Study Skills

1 Words with Similar Meanings. Page 207.

As you go over the instructions, point out that the words in the exercise cannot be substituted for each other in many cases. Have students work in

Chapter 9

pairs to complete the exercise. Remind them to check in a dictionary if they are not sure. Go over the answers and ask volunteers to use the words in different sentences to highlight their different meanings.

Answers: 1. c 2. a 3. b 4. b 5. c 6. a 7. c 8. b 9. a 10. c 11. a 12. b

2 Categories (Content Areas). Page 208.

Read the instructions and example together. Point out the one word that has a more general meaning than the others. Have students complete the exercise. As you go over the answers, have volunteers explain the general meaning of the one word and tell how it includes the other words.

Sample Answers: 2. a very young child 3. medical professions   4. parts of the brain 5. verbs for consuming or using things 6. health problems   7. physical characteristics 8. school subjects

3 Word Roots and Affixes. Page 209.

Read aloud the prefixes, suffixes, and word roots. Ask volunteers to suggest words that contain these parts. Then have students complete the exercise individually without using a dictionary. Go over the answers together. Encourage students to point out the affixes and roots that they used to determine their answers.

Answers: 1. c 2. a 3. d 4. b 5. e 6. d 7. a 8. d

Part 4 Reading in the Real World

1 Summarizing a Passage. Page 211.

Read the suggestions for writing a summary aloud. Point out the steps for restating ideas using different words. Tell students to read the article on page 212 and mark the main ideas and details. Then have students work in small groups to compare their markings.

After You Read

2 Checking Your Understanding. Page 213.

Go over the answers after students have completed the exercise individually. Tell students that their answers to these questions will be important for the next exercise.

Sample Answers:
1. Karl Kim is a graduate student who works with Joy Hirsch, a neuroscientist.
2. They do research in New York City at Memorial Sloan-Kettering Cancer Center.
3. They use a functional magnetic resonance imager.
4. This instrument helps them to see which parts of the brain are more active in different language learners.
5. They studied two groups of people. In the first group, there were people who had learned English as a second language when they were adults. In the second group, there were people who had learned English as a second language when they were children.
6. They looked at Broca's area which is in the left frontal part and Wenicke's area which is in the rear of the brain.
7. They concluded that the same region of the brain (in Broca's area) is used for both languages if the person learned the second language as a child. If an older person learned the second language, then he or she would use a different region (in Broca's area) for the second language.

3 Summarizing. Page 213.

After students have summarized the article using their notes, have volunteers read their summaries to the class.

Sample Answer:
Karl Kim, a graduate student, and Joy Hirsch, a neuroscientist, have been studying which parts of the brain people use when they learn languages. They have been doing research at Memorial Sloan-Kettering Cancer Center in New York. They studied two groups of people:

people who learned English as a second language when they were children and people who learned English as adults. With a functional magnetic resonance imager, they could see which parts of the brain were more active when the people were using their first and second languages. They found that people who learned the second language as children, used the same region of the brain for both their first and second languages. The people who learned as adults, used a different region of the brain for their second language than they used for their first language.

Video Activities: Mapping the Human Genome

Before You Watch

Read the questions aloud and ask students to discuss their answers in small groups. Have volunteers report to the class their answers.

Sample Answers:
1. Genes.
2. A gene is a unit on a chromosome that determines characteristics of the organism. DNA is an acid that is in all living cells. DNA makes up the genes and chromosomes.
3. Answers will vary.

Watch [on video]

Preview the questions before watching the video. Students can discuss their answers in small groups.

Sample Answers:
1. The "book of life" is the map of the chemical sequence for DNA.

2. The scientists are trying to identify the chemicals for the 80,000 genes that are in the human body. Their goal is to figure out which genes lead to different

diseases and then to develop cures for the diseases.

Watch Again [on video]

Call attention to the chart and the headings. Then, replay the video and have students complete the chart. Go over the answers with the whole class.

Sample Answers:

Benefit: genes that lead to disease will be identified; cures for the diseases will be possible

Disadvantage: discrimination; people might use genetic information as reasons for not hiring people for jobs and for not providing health insurance

After You Watch

Remind students to use all the information from the charts and answers to questions in the other video exercises as they prepare their summaries. Students can share their summaries with partners.

Answers will vary.

Medicine, Myths, and Magic

Goals

- **Read and understand ethical questions of modern medicine**
- **Preview a reading selection**
- **Understand main idea**
- **Get meaning from context: logic**
- **Understand reading structure**
- **Make inferences**
- **Understand author's viewpoint**
- **Summarize**
- **Distinguish fact from theory**
- **Apply information**
- **Categorize words**
- **Use appropriate word forms**
- **Understand word roots and affixes**
- **Make predictions**
- **Understand analogies**
- **Scan magazine articles**

Part 1 Medical Technology and Bioethics

Before You Read

1 Getting Started. Page 216.

Ask students to identify people, places, machines, and activities in the photos. Make a list of vocabulary for future reference. Be sure students are familiar with ultrasound and MRI (magnetic resonance imaging). Have students discuss the questions in small groups. Ask volunteers to report their groups' answers.

Sample Answers:

1. Recent discoveries in medical technology include cloning, genetic engineering, and laser surgery.

2. Some possible problems with multiple births might be low birth weight of the infants, not fully developed organs, heart and/or lung problems, limited resources for caring for the infants.

3. A benefit of MRI scans is that a picture can be made of a "slice" of the body. It makes it easier to detect tumors, study the brain, study eye and ear structure, and showing good and abnormal tissues.

4. Extending human life makes it possible for people to be productive for more years. It improves the quality of life for older people. Some problems might be the cost of more medicine and paying for continued health care for older people.

2 Preparing to Read. Page 217.

Read the instructions together, explain how surveying a selection leads to better understanding of it. Then have students complete the exercise. As you go over the answers, have volunteers predict what information they might find under the different subheadings.

Answers:
Topics: 1. — 2. √ 3. √ 4. √ 5. √ 6. √ 7. —

Questions: 1. √ 2. √ 3. — 4. √ 5. √ 6. — 7. √ 8. √

3 Vocabulary Preview. Page 217.

Read aloud the words as students check the ones they don't know. Remind them to look back at this list later after completing the reading selection exercises to check their understand of the new words.

Read

4 Medical Technology and Bioethics. Page 218. [on tape/CD]

Call attention to the guiding question in the instructions. Tell students to think about possible answers to the question as they read and listen to the selection. Then, play the tape or CD and have students follow along in their books. If needed, stop the recording occasionally to check understanding or to point out vocabulary words. Listen and read a second time.

After You Read

5 Getting the Main Ideas. Page 220.

Read the instructions together and have students complete the exercise. Discuss the answers together.

Answers: 1. T 2. I 3. I 4. T 5. F 6. F 7. I

6 Getting Meaning from Context. Page 221.

Have students complete the exercise individually or in pairs. Go over the answers.

Answers: 1. breakthrough 2. diagnose 3. treat 4. extend 5. beneficial 6. surgery 7. value 8. fetus 9. conceiving 10. fertilization 11. transplanting 12. concerns 13. artificial 14. supply 15. hire 16. physicians

Call attention to the instructions and sentence in the second part of the exercise. Remind students to use logic and context clues to complete this part. Review the answers with the group.

Answers: 1. four, five, six 2. three babies, four babies, five babies, six babies

7 Understanding Reading Structure. Page 222.

Read the medical technology in the first column aloud. Then have students complete the matching exercise. Students can compare their answers in

pairs. If they disagree, have them check back in the reading selection.

Answers: 1. c 2. d 3. c 4. e 5. a 6. b 7. d 8. b 9. d 10. d.

8 Making Inferences. Page 222.

Review making inferences as needed, reminding students that an inference is not stated directly. It is an idea that is based on evidence. After students complete the exercise, go over the answers and the supporting information from the selection.

Answers:

1. √ ...there is a new medical breakthrough... leads to more changes... don't have a chance to consider...
2. √ ...the answer reflects each person's ... values.
3. —
4. √ ...when a couple will be able to choose the sex of their child...
5. √ At a cost of over $75,000 for the delivery of one such baby...
6. √ Of course there are ethical concerns...
7. —

9 Viewpoint. Page 223.

Have students refer back to the reading as they consider the author's point of view. Discuss the answer with the entire class.

Sample Answer:

The author believes that there are not enough bioethicists to help doctors and patients find answers to the difficult questions that arise with the new technologies. The answer is for medical schools to include courses in ethics for doctors.

Discussing the Reading

10 Small Group Discussion. Page 223.

Arrange students in groups of five or six to answer the questions about technology and ethics in medicine. Ask a volunteer from each group to share the most interesting items from their groups' discussions.

Answers will vary.

11 Discussing Life Expectancy. Page 224.

Have groups discuss the answers to the questions about the Cross-Cultural Note. Ask groups to share their ideas with the class. Guide students to summarize the information.

Answers will vary.

Talk It Over

Considering Medical Ethics

Before assigning the exercise, go over the vocabulary in the questions: *euthanasia, incurably.* You may want to have students consider the issues as a homework assignment and then share their answers in small groups in the next class. Encourage students to justify and support their responses.

Answers will vary.

12 Checking Your Understanding. Page 224.

Students can complete the exercise individually. Ask students to compare their answers with others in the class. Alternatively, go over the answers with the entire group.

Sample Answers:

1. Some recent discoveries in the field of medical technology are birth control pills, ultrasound and amniocentesis, fertility drugs, *in vitro* fertilization, organ transplants, xenotransplants, bio-synthetics, and MRI scans.

2. The birth control pill has changed society by giving women more choice over their bodies. It has controlled the population growth. It has changed society and the way people think about gender roles, sex, freedom, and family.

4. A negative consequence is that parents in some cultures might make decisions for abortions rather than have daughters.

5. Some new ways for women to become pregnant are with fertility drugs and with *in vitro* fertilization.

7. Technology will help people in the future live longer with organ transplants and by blocking certain genes.

8. To find answers to ethical questions, hospitals hire bioethicists. Medical schools offer courses in ethics for future doctors.

There are some ethical questions that need to be answered because of recent discoveries in medical technology. Have the changes in society that resulted from the birth control pill been a good thing? Should parents be able to choose the sex of their child? When does life begin? Should society have to pay for care of multiple births? What should happen to fertilized eggs not used in *in vitro* fertilization? Should animal organs be used in humans? When is a person dead? How much care should be given to a dying patient? Who should pay for expensive medical tests and technology?

Beyond the Text

Encourage students to look for recent newspaper, magazine, or Internet articles related to medical ethics and new medical technological breakthroughs. Students can share their findings with the class and give their own personal reactions to the articles.

Part 2 The Mind-Body Relationship

1 Main Idea and Summary. Page 225. [on tape/CD]

Read the instructions for the exercise together. Review as needed main idea and summaries. You may want to have students work in pairs to complete the exercise. You may want to play the tape or CD as students follow along in their books. Ask volunteers to share their answers and summaries with the class. Point out common features and information in the responses.

Sample Answers:
B Main Idea: The effectiveness of a medicine depends partly on what the patients expect the medicine to do.
Summary: If a patient hopes that a drug will help, then the drug will more likely have that effect. Doctors have seen in studies that if patients expect a result from a drug, then it often has the desired result.

C Main Idea: The brain can produce its own natural "drug."
Summary: Studies have shown that the brain releases natural chemicals which are like drugs. The more a patient believes in the doctor or treatment, the more natural chemicals the brain releases. So the patient postively affects his or her own health.

D Main Idea: A pleasant environment can help a person get better.
Summary: A bright and cheerful environment seems to make patients recover more quickly. After several months, some patients (who had been in a sad, colorless environment) become well in a bright and cheerful environment.

E Main Idea: Doctors think there is a link between a person's mind and the risk of cancer.
Summary: Studies show that people who express their emotions are healthier than people who don't show their feelings. Cancer patients who didn't show their feelings had cancer return more often than patients who expressed their feelings.

After You Read

2 Distinguishing Facts from Theories. Page 227.
Review words and expressions associated with statements of fact and theory. Then have students complete the exercise. As you go over the

answers, have volunteers point out parts of the reading selection that support their responses.

Answers: 1. Theory 2. Theory 3. Fact 4. Theory 5. Fact 6. Theory 7. Theory

3 Applying Information. Page 227.
Read the instructions together. Then have students complete the exercise. Students can compare their answers with others in the class.

Sample Answers:
1. Hope for a cure; believe the medicine will work
2. Stay in a bright, cheerful room or place
3. Don't be afraid to express your feelings

Discussing the Reading

4 Small Group Discussion. Page 227.
Point out the chart on page 228. Go over the ailments listed on the chart as needed. Ask students to suggest other possible conditions or ailments to include in the bottom row of the chart. Read the instructions and steps in the exercise together. Allow 15-20 minutes for students to interview each other or groups of students about folk cures. Have students compare their charts in small groups. Ask a volunteer from each group to report the similarities and differences that they noted on their charts. Talk about advantages and disadvantages of drugstore medicine and traditional cures. You may want to have students prepare a written summary of their charts and answers to the questions in #2.

Part 3 Building Vocabulary and Study Skills

1 Categories. Page 229.
Have students work individually on the categorization activity. Then have students compare their answers with others in the class. Go over the answers with the entire group. You

may want to have volunteers suggest other words that might belong in the given categories.

Answers:
1. liver, kidney, throat
2. anger, sadness, hatred
3. insomnia, headache, ulcer
4. infection, bacteria, genetics
5. ultrasound
6. organization, tribe, community, society
7. colony, village, cave
8. values, ethics, morals
9. hug, grin, shout
10. landlocked, harbor, tropical
11. diagnosis, treatment, surgery

2 Word Forms. Page 230.

Read the instructions together. You may want to have volunteers suggest some forms using the base in the exercise. For example: *heal: health, healthy, healing, healed, healthful, unhealthy.* Then have students complete the exercise. Go over the responses.

Sample Answers: 1. diagnosis (treatment, healing) 2. combination 3. traditional 4. diagnosis 5. participation, healer 6. effectiveness 7. acceptable

3 Word Roots and Affixes. Page 230.

Read the prefixes, suffixes, and word roots aloud. Ask volunteers to suggest words that contain these affixes and roots. Students can complete the exercise individually. Go over the answers together. Encourage students to point out the affixes and roots that they used to determine their answers.

Answers: 1. c 2. e 3. d 4. b 5. c 6. a 7. c 8. e 9. c

4 Improving Reading Skills: Predictions. Page 232.

Read the instructions together. Point out the example. Remind students to use context clues to guess what the last word should be. Have

students time themselves for each of the groups. Go over the answers.

Answers: 2. pa<u>tient</u> 3. eth<u>ical</u> 4. physi<u>cian</u> 5. break<u>through</u> 6. tri<u>plets</u> 7. or<u>gans</u> 8. ener<u>gy</u> 9. phy<u>sical</u> 10. so<u>lution</u>

Explain that there may be more than one possible answer in this exercise. Remind students that this is a timed exercise, so they should work ask quickly as possible. Go over possible answers.

Sample Answers: 1. germs, bacteria, viruses 2. questions, concerns, dilemmas 3. patients, diseases, illnesses 4. headaches, pains, fevers 5. holistic healing, folk cures 6. minds, emotional problems 7. calm, quiet, passive 8. disease, depression 9. angry, frustrated, annoyed 10. feelings, emotions

Focus on Testing

Understanding Analogies
Read the tips together. Refer back to Chapter 8 for specific relationships commonly used in analogies. Call attention to the example and its explanation. Then have students complete the exercise. As you go over the answers, have volunteers point out the clues they used to make their answers.

Answers: 1. c 2. a 3. d 4. c 5. c 6. b

Part 4 Reading in the Real World

1 Scanning Magazine Articles. Page 235.
As you read aloud the instructions, call attention to the title and subheadings of the magazine article. Have students make predictions about the content of the article. Point out the questions in

Exercise 2. Remind students to use these questions to guide their reading of the article and to determine the main ideas. Then have students read the selection.

2 Application. Page 236.

Students can complete the exercise individually and then compare their answers with others in the class. Go over the answers with the whole group. Encourage students to share any experiences they have had with these cures or other home remedies they know for the conditions.

Answers: 1. garlic 2. ginger capsules, ginger tea 3. acupressure 4. baking soda in water

3 Getting Meaning from Context. Page 237.

After students have completed the exercise individually, go over the answers. Ask volunteers to use the words and phrases in sentences.

Answers: 1. side effects 2. soak 3. after effects 4. germs 5. nausea, queasiness 6. endorphins

Beyond the Text

If students are interested, have them look for articles related to medical and health issues. Students can present their findings to the class and share new vocabulary they have learned.

Video Activities: A New Treatment for Back Pain

Before You Watch

Read the questions aloud and ask students to discuss their answers in small groups. Have students report to the class their answers.

Sample Answers:
1. Answers will vary. 2. Answers will vary. 3. Nerve = a part of the body that carries messages from the brain to the different parts of the body; spinal cord = the large cord of nerve tissue that goes through the backbone up to the brain; brain = the large mass of nerve tissue in the skull; Information reach the brain through a system of nerves. The individual nerves send information to the spinal cord and up to the brain.

Watch [on video]

Preview the questions before viewing the video. As students watch, have them decide if the statements are true or false. Go over the answers together and ask volunteers to correct the false statements to make them true.

Answers: 1. T 2. F 3. F 4.F

Watch Again [on video]

Call attention to the chart and the headings. Then, replay the video and have students complete the chart. Go over the answers with the whole class.

Sample Answers:
Doris Dorry: During/After Treatment: a lot of relief

Judy Ellis: Before Treatment: pain, hopeless; had 3 surgical procedures on her back; During/After Treatment: relaxing, can fall asleep, hopeful

After You Watch

Students can work in pairs to arrange the steps in proper order. If needed, students can watch the video again. Go over the answers with the group. You may want to have students prepare their own list of steps to describe a medical procedure or treatment for a specific ailment.

Answers: 3, 2, 7, 5, 1, 4, 6

Chapter 11

The Media

Goals

- **Read and understand newspapers**
- **Preview a reading selection**
- **Understand main idea**
- **Get meaning from context**
- **Make inferences**
- **Understand chronology**
- **Understand author's viewpoint**
- **Understand figurative language**
- **Skim for main ideas**
- **Summarize**
- **Distinguish facts from opinions**
- **Understand the grammar of newspaper headlines**
- **Understand newspaper language**
- **Use hyphenated words**
- **Scan newspaper articles**

Part 1 How To Read a Newspaper

Before You Read

1 **Getting Started. Page 240.**
You might want to bring in some samples of local newspapers for students to look at the use as resources. Ask volunteers to describe the photos on page 240. List vocabulary on the board. Arrange students in groups to discuss the questions. After 10-15 minutes, have volunteers report their groups' responses.

Sample Answers:
1. You can learn about the news by watching TV news programs, listening to radio news reports, reading newspapers, reading news magazines, reading news on the Internet. I prefer....
2. Answers will vary.
3. Answers will vary.

2 **Preparing to Read. Page 241.**
Have students complete the exercise after reviewing the purpose of surveying a reading selection. As you go over the answers, have volunteers predict what information they might find in the selection.

Answers: 1. √ 2. — 3. √ 4. √ 5. — 6. √ 7. — 8. √ 9. — 10. √

3 **Vocabulary Preview. Page 241.**
Tell students to check words they don't know on the list as you read them aloud. Remind them to look back at this list later after completing the reading selection exercises to check their understand of the new words.

Read

4 **How to Read a Newspaper. Page 242. [on tape/CD]**
Point out the guiding question as you read aloud the instructions. Encourage students to use the question to guide them as they read the selection. Play the tape or CD and have students follow along in their books. Pause the recording occasionally to check understanding and to point out vocabulary words. Then, listen a second time.

After You Read

5 Getting the Main Ideas. Page 245.

Review "stated" and "implied" information. Then have students complete the exercise. Discuss the answers together.

Answers: 1. √ 2. — 3. √ 4. √ 5. √
6. √ 7. — 8. √ 9. — 10. √

6 Getting Meaning from Context. Page 245.

Have students complete the exercise individually or in pairs. Go over the answers.

Answers: 1. kill two birds with one stone
2. doorstep 3. pitcher 4. tabloid
5. yellow 6. op-ed 7. editorials
8. headline 9. customized 10. mug

7 Making Inferences. Page 246.

Remind students to check back in the reading selection as they look for clues about the author of the reading selection. Point out that the information will not be stated directly. Go over the answers and supporting information that students used to make their inferences.

Answers:

1. Female; Support: ...my husband and I...

2. teacher of English; Support: ...you ask me for... to learn this language...

3. students learning English; Support: you must... learn this language...

4. informal; Support: "you" ... Let me assure you...

8 Understanding Chronology. Page 246.

Review time expressions as needed. Have students look for examples of the time expressions in the reading selection. Students can complete the exercise individually and then compare their answers with others in the class. Ask volunteers to give the suggestions in proper order. Discuss any differences in order.

Answers: 4, 1, 3, 2, 5, 9, 8, 6, 7

9 Viewpoint. Page 247.

Have students refer back to the reading as they fill in the author's opinions about the topics. Discuss the answers with the entire class, encouraging students to point out specific references that support their responses.

Answers: 1. is challenging 2. is not practical or efficient 3. are not newspapers; are terrible 4. should be objective; facts, not opinions 5. is clearly separated
6. is difficult to understand; is different from "normal" English

10 Checking Your Understanding. Page 247.

After students answer the questions, go over the answers and discuss any variations.

Sample Answers:

1. You can improve your vocabulary by reading an English-language newspaper.

3. A bad newspaper is full of gossip, half-truths, and trash.

4. Some good English-language newspapers are the *Christian Science Monitor*, the *International Herald Tribune*, *USA Today*, *The Bangkok Post*, *The London Times*, and *The Chicago Tribune*.

6. A newspaper usually has the following sections: hard news (Global, National, Local), Op-Ed, Classified ads, Entertainment, Business, and Sports.

8. You can read the newspaper quickly if you throw away section that you aren't interested in, preview the rest of the newspaper by looking over the sections, read headlines on the front page, choose five articles, read the first paragraph or two (more if you are really interested). You should also guess meaning from context.

9. You can use the computer to find the news with online news services. It will search for topics you are interested in.

10. You can find a newspaper that avoids subjects you're not interested in by using a customized online news service.

Discussing the Reading

11 Small Group Discussion. Page 247.
Arrange students in groups of five or six to answer the questions about newspapers. Ask a volunteer from each group to share the most interesting items from their groups' discussions.

Answers will vary.

Beyond the Text

Ask students to follow the steps in the reading selection as they read an English-language newspaper. Have them share their experiences in class. Students can complete one of the projects.

Focus on Testing

Figurative Language
Read the instructions together, pointing out the differences between literal and figurative meanings. Present other examples of words with literal and figurative meanings as needed. After students complete the exercise, go over the answers with the class. Ask volunteers to justify their responses.

Answers: 1. b 2. b 3. b 4. d 5. a

Part 2 The Daily News

1 Skimming for Main Ideas. Page 249.
Read the instructions aloud. Then have students complete the exercise individually. Go over the answers together.

Answers: 1. D 2. A 3. F 4. C 5. E. 6. B

2 Summarizing. Page 249. [on tape/CD]
Play the tape or CD as students follow along in their books. Students can write their summarizing statements on a separate piece of paper. Have students compare their summaries with others in the class and make adjustments to their own statements as needed. Review possible statements with the whole class.

Sample Answers:

A. The chief of police's decision to have the police department check on possible police misconduct does not seem like a good idea. An outside group should investigate not the police.

B. Kevin Brisbane helped his team, the Supernovas, defeat the Jaguars last night.

C. The last show of "Survivor" was last night. Although the writer thinks it is a terrible program, similar programs are being planned for the future.

D. Three men hijacked an airplane in Seoul. There are 92 passengers and 7 crew members on the plane still. They want one million dollars.

E. The Hours, a novel by Michael Cunningham, tells about the lives of three women in different settings.

F. A good host makes the guests feel comfortable, so it would be all right for a guest to help in the kitchen.

After You Read

3 Distinguishing Facts from Opinions. Page 251.
Read the instructions together, pointing out the differences between facts and opinions. Call attention to the words often used with opinions. Then have students decide if the statements are facts or opinions. Go over the answers, asking volunteers to explain.

Answers: 3. O 4. F 5. O 6. O 7. F 8. F 9. F 10. F 11. F 12. F 13. O 14. O

Discussing the Reading

4 Small Group Discussion. Page 252.
Read the questions aloud, explaining vocabulary as needed. Then arrange students in small groups to discuss their responses. After 10-15 minutes, have volunteers report to the class the most interesting comments and points of their discussions.

Part 3 Building Vocabulary and Study Skills

1 The Grammar of Newspaper Headlines. Page 252.
Read the grammar rules for headlines aloud. Point out the examples, making sure students understand how to interpret the headlines. In pairs, have students restate the headlines using complete sentences. Go over the answers.

Sample Answers:
1. Elvis Presley has been seen in a bus station.
2. Medical technology is the topic of a meeting in Tokyo.
3. Hikers have found ancient paintings in a cave in Spain.
4. The UN has sent aid to the flood victims.
5. A new planet has been discovered.
6. Two hostages were shot. One has died.
7. Thailand and Mexico are going to sign a trade agreement.
8. A TV show, which began in Sweden, is now popular worldwide.
9. The critics have claimed that the police chief was covering up errors.
10. A boy was injured by a truck; the driver has been arrested.

2 Newspaper Language. Page 254.
Read together the list of newspaper language with their figurative meanings. Have students

refer to this list and to the grammar rules from Exercise 1 as they complete the exercise. Go over the answers with the class.

Sample Answers:
1. A study has linked moods to (a person's) diet.
2. Smoking has been prohibited now in city restaurants.
3. "A tax increase is necessary," the mayor has declared.
4. The city council has approved the tax increase.
5. The results of the police investigation have been released.
6. The President is supporting a microlending program in rural areas. He is searching for funds.
7. The mother of a girl who was killed in the park is looking for help.
8. The arrest of a local man has initiated anger.
9. A study has found that the high rate of diabetes is connected to diet.
10. Students have been choosing technology majors.

3 Hyphenated Words. Page 255.
Point out the examples of hyphens. Have volunteers give other examples of hyphenated words and usage of hyphens. Then have students complete the exercise individually. Go over the answers together.

Answers: 1. seven-member, two-day
2. right-hand, op-ed 3. modern-day, old-fashioned 4. English language, half-truths

Beyond the Text

Ask students to look for newspaper headlines. Students can share their headlines in small groups and translate them into complete sentences.

Part 4 Reading in the Real World

1 Vocabulary. Page 256.

Read the tips on vocabulary together. Remind students that it is not necessary to know the meaning of every word in a selection to understand the main ideas and important points. Students need to be able to identify the important words that are critical to understanding and look those words up as needed. Call attention to the list of words and expressions that will be in the Exercise 2. You may want to read aloud the words and discuss their meanings. Then go on to the next exercise.

2 Scanning a Magazine Article. Page 257.

Tell students to read the questions in Exercise 3 before they begin the reading selection. After students have completed reading the selection, have them identify the main ideas.

After You Read

3 Checking Your Answers. Page 258.

After students have completed the exercise individually, go over the answers.

Sample Answers:
1. It means that the newspaper changed from Communist-oriented news to gossip and tabloid-style newspapers.
2. The nude photos made the newspaper popular so people wanted to buy it.
3. e
4. c
5. c
6. e
7. Newspapers in China needed to change to become financially self-supporting. They did this by changing the content of the newspapers to more gossip and entertainment-oriented stories.

Talk It Over

Censorship

Students can discuss the topic of censorship in small groups. Have volunteers report to the class the opinions and ideas from their groups. Help summarize the ideas discussed.

Video Activities: Bye, Bye, Charlie Brown

Before You Watch

Read the questions aloud and ask students to discuss their answers in small groups. Have students report to the class their answers.

Answers will vary.

Watch [on video]

Before watching the video, have students read the questions. Have students fill in answers to the questions. Go over the answers together.

Answers:
1. He didn't like the name because it had no dignity.
2. Charles Schultz retired because it was hard to meet the daily deadlines while he was fighting cancer.
3. Charles Schultz announced his retirement and in his final appearance in newspapers, he thanked his fans and editors.

Watch Again [on video]

Ask students to read the statements in this exercise to guide them as they watch the video again. After you replay the video, have students fill in the missing details. Go over the answers with the whole class.

Answers:

1. 50; 2,600; 75; 355,000,000; 1950
2. dignity; Charlie Brown or Snoopy
3. Lucy

After You Watch

Students can discuss their answers to the
questions in small groups. Students may want to
bring in samples of their favorite cartoon strips to
share with their groups or the whole class.

With Liberty and Justice for All

Part 1 The Concept of Law

Before You Read

1 Getting Started. Page 262.
Have volunteers describe the photo on page 262. List key vocabulary on the board. Then arrange students in groups to discuss the questions. After 10-15 minutes, have volunteers report their groups' responses.

Sample Answers:
1. The scene takes place in a courtroom. There is a judge, a witness, a jury, lawyers (prosecuting and defense), defendant, and plaintiff, court stenographer, and bailiff. The bailiff is swearing in a witness. The jury and judge are listening to the proceedings. The judge is checking that the trial is fair. The prosecutor is explaining the problem and trying to prove that the defendant is guilty. The defense is trying to show that the defendant is innocent. The stenographer is taking notes on everything that is said in the trial.

2. Before this scene, there was a chance for lawyers from both sides to present an overview of their sides. The jury had to be selected before that.

   Next the lawyers from both sides will ask the witness questions. When all the witnesses have been questioned, the lawyers will summarize their sides and the jury will decide if the defendant is guilty or not.

3. Answers will vary.

2 Preparing to Read. Page 262.
Read aloud the instructions. Stress the importance of preparing questions and looking for answers in active reading. Have students compare their questions with others in the class.

Sample Answers:
1. What happens in a court trial?
2. What kinds of laws are decided in courtrooms?
3. What is the meaning of "law"?
4. What are different types of laws?
5. Do laws prevent crimes?
6. Who decides questions of laws?
7. What are the differences between modern and traditional justice?

3 Vocabulary Preview. Page 263.
Have students check the words they don't know as you read the vocabulary list aloud. Remind them to look back at this list later after completing the reading selection exercises to check their understand of the new words.

Read

**4 The Concept of Law. Page 263.
[on tape/CD]**
Remind students to think about their questions
from Exercise 2 as they read the selection. Play
the tape or CD and have students follow along in
their books. Pause the recording from time to
time to check understanding and to point out
vocabulary words. Then, listen a second time.

After You Read

5 Getting the Main Ideas. Page 265.
Have students complete the exercise. Discuss the
answers together and have volunteers point out
references from the reading that support their
answers.

Answers: 1. F 2. I 3. F 4. T 5. I 6. I

6 Finding Important Details. Page 265.
Go over the instructions, clarifying as needed.
Point out the sample statement. Then have
students write seven more examples of concepts
of justice for the different societies. Students can
exchange books and try to identify the societies
for each of the details. Students can go over their
answers together.

Sample Answers:

(J, TS) 2. Punishment is not believed to be a
deterrent.

(J) 3. It is important to restore the balance
through the justice system.

(US) 4. There is a big difference between "sins"
and "crimes."

(TS) 5. There is little separation between
customs, laws, and religious beliefs.

(US) 6. Personal and individual justice are very
important.

(US) 7. Civil law is a big business.

(J) 8. Social harmony (peaceful agreement) is
more important than individual rights.

(TS) 9. A person who is believed to have
supernatural power might judge disputes.

(TS) 10. Family leaders or village
representatives might decide disputes.

**7 Understanding Vocabulary from Context.
Page 266.**
Students can check back in the reading selection
for the vocabulary words and use context clues
to guess the meanings. Go over the answers and
ask volunteers to explain how they decided on
the meanings of the words.

Sample Answers: 1. Idea 2. A penalty
for a crime 3. Fair treatment 4. Something
that prevents an action 5. To do (a crime)
6. To put back in the original state
7. A peaceful and calm condition 8. A break
in a religious law 9. To break a law
10. A case that is in a court to be decided
11. To start legal proceedings against someone
12. A feeling of peace and agreement
13. A disagreement or argument
14. The decision of a judge or court case

8 Understanding Outlines. Page 266.
Review the purpose and format of an outline as
needed. Have students complete their own
outlines and then share them with others in the
class. Discuss any major differences in the
outlines.

Sample Answers:

II.   A. In Western culture
      1. Punishing to prevent the committing of additional crimes
      2. Fear of punishment keeps others from doing crimes
      B. In non-Western cultures
      1. Punishment is not a deterrent
      2. Need to restore balance in a situation

III. A. In Western culture
      1. "laws" are different from "customs"
      2. "crimes" different from "sins"
      B. In non-Western cultures
      1. in some, there is little separation between customs, laws, and religious belief
      2. in others, these are separate, but still are different from those in the West
      3. a crime in one country may be acceptable in another country

IV.   A. Criminal laws for murder or theft
      B. Civil system for violation of other people's rights
      1. In US, individual justice is important to many civil lawsuits
      2. In Japan, social harmony is important so agreements are made outside of courtroom

V.   A. In courts
      1. A judge chosen by the government
      2. A jury, or group of people
      B. In tribal societies
      1. a person with special power settles disputes

VI.   A. In societies where courts and judges don't exist
      1. Self-help: friends and family settle disagreements
      2. Social disapproval, opinions of others in the town

VII. A. In Tanzania
      1. Family leaders or village representatives try to settle disputes
      2. If cannot be settled, then case goes to modern court
      B. In Washington State
      1. Judge sent youths to tribal court for punishment
      2. Tribe set up punishment

9 Checking Your Understanding. Page 268.

Have students go back and answer their questions from Exercise 2. Students can check in the reading selection. It is possible that some of their questions were not answered. You may want to have students share their questions and answers in small groups.

Answers will vary depending on students' questions.

Discussing the Reading

10 Small Group Discussion. Page 268.

Arrange students in groups of five or six to answer the questions about systems of justice. Ask a volunteer from each group to share the most interesting items from their groups' discussions.

Answers will vary.

Beyond the Text

Students can search for interesting articles related to trials. Ask students to read and summarize the articles and share interesting points with the class.

Part 2 The Legal System in the News

1 Skimming for Main Ideas. Page 268. [on tape/CD]

Read the instructions aloud. Then play the tape or CD as students follow along in their books. Have students complete the exercise individually. Go over the answers together.

Sample Answers:
1. A McDonald's customer caused a traffic accident while eating and driving. The victim sued McDonald's, but the court says McDonald's in not responsible for the accident.
2. A tribal court in Papua New Guinea decided that a woman was part of a payment to restore harmony to another family. The National Court system decided that she is a free woman and cannot be given away like a possession.
3. Phoolan Devis, a former criminal and later elected politician, was to be arrested for murders committed in 1981. She claims she is innocent, but disappeared before she was arrested.

After You Read

2 Summarizing. Page 270.

After students complete their headlines, have them share them with others in the class. As a class decide on the best headline for each article.

Sample Answers:
A: McDonald's Not Responsible for Accident

B: National Court Decides Woman Is Not Part of Payment

C: Bandit Queen/Politician Disappears As Police Come to Arrest Her

3 Making Inferences. Page 270.

Read together the instructions, pointing out that students need to make guesses based on the information in the articles. Students can work in pairs or small groups. Then ask volunteers to share the inferences from their groups. Have others point out information from the articles that support their inferences.

Sample Answers:
1. In the US, people can sue companies if consumers do something wrong when using the companies' products.
2. In Papua New Guinea, the National Court can overrule a tribe. In tribal customs, women do not have personal rights or freedom.
3. In India, it may be difficult for some people of certain social classes to get fair court hearings.

Discussing the Reading

4 Small Group Discussion. Page 271.

Read the questions aloud, pointing out key vocabulary. Call attention to the Cross-Cultural Note about legal history. If students are familiar with some of the systems, ask them to explain what they know about them. Then, allow 15-20 minutes for small group discussion of the questions. Ask volunteers from each group to report to the class their ideas and answers to these questions.

Part 3 Building Vocabulary and Study Skills

1 Categories (Content Areas). Page 272.

Ask volunteers to suggest words that might belong in each of the categories: education, religion, medical, law, and business. Call attention to the category abbreviations to be used in the exercise. Have students complete the exercise individually and then compare their answers with partners. Then, go over the answers with the whole class.

Answers: 1. edu 2. law 3. med 4. bus
5. law 6. edu 7. law 8. law 9. rel
10. bus 11. med 12. rel 13. rel
14. med 15. med 16. bus 17. bus
18. law 19. med 20. bus 21. rel
22. edu 23. law 24. edu 25. law
26. edu 27. law/edu 28. edu 29. edu/rel
30. bus 31. med 32. law 33. bus
34. rel 35. med 36. law 37. bus 38. rel
39. bus/law 40. edu 41. bus 42. law
43. bus 44. med 45. edu 46. med
47. law

2 Content Area Vocabulary. Page 272.

Explain the activity by reading together the directions. Have groups write on large pieces of paper or on sections of the board. Allow about 5 minutes for a category group. Ask a volunteer from each group to present their words. Give a point for each word that fits in the category. Have several round using a different category group each time.

Answers will vary.

3 Improving Reading Skills: Prediction. Page 273.

Read the instructions aloud. You may want to have students look back through the chapter to review vocabulary related to laws and legal systems. Then have students complete the exercise. Go over the possible answers with the class.

Sample Answers:
1. Settlement/agreement
2. advisable
3. Finding/Selecting/Choosing
4. suggestions/recommendations
5. similar
6. resources
7. names/lawyers/attorneys

8. knows
9. problem/legal issue
10. step
11. set up/ arrange
12. meeting/appointment
13. questions/issues
14. procedures/practices
15. feeling/response
16. a fee/anything
17. determine/decide
18. case/problem/question
19. billing/charging
20. expenses/extra costs
21. letters
22. papers/forms
23. money/time
24. visit/meet
25. list
26. points
27. carefully
28. be
29. lawyer/attorney
30. facts/information
31. papers/information

4 Missing Words. Page 273.

As you read the instructions together, point out that students will be preparing their own exercise similar to Exercise 3. Have students work in groups or as a whole class to suggest words to complete the passages.

Part 4 Reading in the Real World

Focus on Testing

Timed Tests
Read the tips on taking timed tests together. Remind students to preview any reading

selection by looking at title, subtitle, and questions to guide them as they read. Go over the answers for the first set of questions before having students complete the second reading selection and questions.

Answers: 1. b 2. a 3. d 4. c 5. d
6. d 7. d 8. e 9. d 10. e

Video Activities: Justice and Racism

Before You Watch
Read the vocabulary words aloud and have volunteers give the meanings of words they know. Ask students to find the meanings of the other words in dictionaries. Encourage students to think about when and where these words might be used.

Answers:
justice = fair treatment according to the law

jury = a group of people who swear that they will listen to the court case and help decide the outcome of the case

defendant = a person who has been accused of doing a crime or something wrong

guilty = having done something wrong; not innocent

verdict = the decision made at the end of a trial

convict = to prove that someone is responsible for a crime or wrongdoing

testimony = the evidence or statement that a witness gives in a trial

Watch [on video]
Before watching the video, have students read the questions. After the video, have students discuss their answers in small groups. Ask volunteers to report their groups' answers.

Sample Answers:
1. There seems to be a different set of rules in the justice system for people of different races. Racial bias is part of the society and the court system.
2. The juries are more racist because judge has an ethical obligation to see and eliminate any bias in the court system.
3. The solution to the problem is knowledge, awareness, and education. It needs to be in people's minds so they are prepared to look for it.

Chapter 1

Watch Again [on video]

Ask students to read the statements in this exercise to guide them as they watch the video again. After you replay the video, have students fill in the missing words. Go over the answers with the whole class.

Answers:

a. system b. Jurors; jurors c. obligation
d. marching

After You Watch

Students can talk about the meanings of the words and to look them up in dictionaries as needed. Have groups present their meanings and sentences to the class for further discussion.

Sample Answers:

bias = a partiality or slight inclination towards one side

The defendant is my cousin, so I may be biased in my view of the case.

racism = a program of practice of discrimination, segregation, or persecution based on a person's race

Racism can result in a qualified person not getting a job because of his or her racial background.

prejudice = an opinion formed without all the facts, usually it is unfavorable

The neighbors didn't know much about new family in town, but they were prejudiced against them because they spoke with a different accent.

apartheid = a policy of strict racial segregation and discrimination against native Africans and other non-white people in South Africa

Reading Placement Test

Part 1 Determining Meaning and Usage from Context

Circle the letter of the best word or words to complete each sentence.

Example:

Public schools are forbidden to teach _____, whereas parochial schools are required to do so.

    a. religious

    b. spiritual

    c. mathematics

    (d.) religion

1. The puppy was very _____ with the children.

    a. calmness

    b. calm

    c. calamity

    d. calms

2. The father harshly _____ every boy who went out with his daughter.

    a. judge

    b. judging

    c. to judge

    d. judged

3. The patient was extremely _____ and had to be subdued.

    a. agitated

    b. agitates

    c. agitating

    d. agitate

4. **Children who wish to _____ or achieve greatness must have drive and work hard.**

   a. drive a car

   b. fail

   c. excel

   d. go home

5. **Poodles, German Shepherds, Golden Retrievers are different types of _____.**

   a. canines

   b. felines

   c. dogs

   d. a and c

6. **If you are having trouble logging onto the Internet you might want to check out your _____.**

   a. modem configuration string

   b. video monitor

   c. word processing program

   d. none of the above

7. **Spending time reading newspapers and _____ is a good way to keep up with current events.**

   a. historical novels

   b. ancient texts

   c. classic books

   d. other periodicals

8. **The enlightened ministers, Catholic priests, Jewish rabbis, and Buddhist monks _____.**

   a. belong to an ecumenical organization

   b. belong to the same denomination

   c. had identical religious training

   d. none of the above is possible

9. **She was a very _____ young child who could read university texts by the time that she was nine years old.**

   a. precocious

   b. illiterate

   c. developmentally delayed

   d. inadequate

10. **The mechanic was confident and felt that it was very _____ or plausible to get the truck repaired in a week.**

    a. unpredictable

    b. unrealistic

    c. feasible

    d. surreal

Part 2 Idiomatic Expressions

Circle the letter of the best meaning of the underlined idiomatic expression.

Example:

She wanted to leave under good terms and not to <u>burn her bridges</u>.

   a. make it impossible to return because of bad feelings

   b. destroy the bridges where she had traveled previously

   c. dynamite a bridge

   d. create bridges and avenues to the future

1. **The mother told her son to be conservative and mindful of what he had since <u>a bird in the hand is worth two in the bush</u>.**

   a. Birds fly away even when you have them in your hand.

   b. Birds are worth watching and loving: the more the merrier.

   c. It is better to hold onto something you own than to leave it unattended, and rush off to try to get something unknown.

   d. Always be conservative and never go after something new.

2. **Carl's boss was against all of Carl's plans for improvement and <u>tied his hands</u>, which prevented him from doing anything innovative.**

   a. was very proactive and supportive of Carl

   b. stopped him from working well

   c. put Carl into a psychiatric hospital where straitjackets were used

   d. Carl put his boss in a straitjacket

3. **Cynthia's father adored her and <u>considered her to be the apple of his eye</u>.**

   a. felt that his daughter could find lots of apples in the trees because she had such good eyes

   b. did everything he could think of to find apples for his daughter

   c. believed that his daughter needed to eat apples to improve her eyes

   d. believed his daughter was wonderful

4. **George was mediocre at many different things; he was <u>a jack of all trades and master of none</u>.**

   a. able to do many things that women could never do

   b. a master of many trades and did many things very well

   c. could do many different things, but none especially well

   d. a master of many things and did everything except one exceptionally well

5. **She wanted to be promoted, but her hopes were <u>dashed</u> when her employer declared bankruptcy.**

   a. dreams were fulfilled

   b. depression was deferred

   c. specific wishes were no longer possible

   d. life became joyful

Part 3 Scanning for Members of Word Families

Circle the letter of the best word to complete each sentence:

Example:

_____ is a noun meaning "a place that sells baked goods."

   a. Baker

   (b.) Bakery

   c. Baked

   d. Bakes

1. _____ is a verb meaning "to become more economical."

   a. Economize

   b. Economical

   c. Economics

   d. Economically

2. _____ is a noun meaning that "someone or something has grown fully or fully developed."

   a. Mature

   b. Maturity

   c. Maturing

   d. Matured

3. _____ is a verb meaning "to take an idea or concept and apply it in other situations."

   a. Extrapolation

   b. Extricate

   c. Extrication

   d. Extrapolate

4. _____ is a noun meaning "a person who tells jokes or funny stories."

   a. Comics

   b. Comedy

   c. Comedian

   d. Comical

5. _____ is a an adjective referring to "the cells of an unborn baby."

   a. Embryo

   b. Embryonic

   c. Embryos

   d. Amoeba

Part 4 Reading Comprehension

Reading 1

Have you ever thought about where you should sit on an airplane? It is important to book your seat early so that you can select a seat that best serves your needs. Individuals traveling in first class and business class usually need to think about whether they want an aisle seat or to sit next to a window or next to the bulkhead, or wall.

If you are stuck in the economy section of the aircraft you must still consider whether you want a window, aisle, or a seat next the bulkhead. You must also take into account many different factors. You should decide whether or not you want to be in the front or rear section of the aircraft. The advantage of being near the front of the plane is that you will be able to board and deplane quickly. However, if you want to get an empty seat next to you, you should get a seat towards the rear, since people are assigned seats from the front to the rear. Please don't be discouraged if you end up with a center or middle seat since most airlines have middle seats that are a little bit wider than the window or aisle seats.

Based on the article, indicate whether each statement is true or false.

Example:

_____ **This short article was written by someone who is unfamiliar with air travel.**

1. ___ A bulkhead is not considered to be a wall.

2. ___ This article is about seat selection in both the economy and business or first class sections of an airplane.

3. ___ According to the article, if you are sitting in the economy section of a plane, you always want to sit towards the front of the section.

4. ___ Seats are assigned from the rear of the aircraft forward.

5. ___ You should be very upset if you get a middle seat.

Reading 2

Have you ever wanted to do something tremendous and earth shattering? You might think that you need to discover a cure for cancer, construct a huge monument, or be the first to fly around the world in a hot air balloon for your activity to count as being remarkable. Actually there are many very simple acts of kindness that can completely save a person's heart or life. My sister was recently touring Germany when she received some very devastating news. It was probably the worst news of her life. She was completely alone, in a strange land with no friends or family. A stranger, a big-sister-type figure, took her in and offered her both an ear and a cup of Earl Grey tea. That simple act gave my sister some of the courage that she needed to tackle her troubles. So the next time you want to do something great, simply take time to be kind to your fellow man or woman.

Based on the article, indicate whether each statement is true or false.

Example:

___ **We know for a fact that the author had a sister and a brother.**

1. ___ If something is earth shattering, it is unimportant.

2. ___ A cure for cancer is noteworthy.

3. ___ Simple acts are never great acts.

4. ___ The author's sister was given some very bad news while she was traveling.

5. ___ The stranger didn't offer the author's sister Earl Grey tea.

Reading 3

The Visually Impaired

Individuals who are blind, or those who are low vision, as well as those with less severe visual impairments, have benefited from a variety of key developments that have occurred in Europe and the United States during the past couple of centuries. Low vision refers to individuals who have very limited sight and it does not have anything to do with whether items are high or low to the ground. The effort to assist the visually challenged began in the latter 1700s, when a gentleman by the name of Victor Hauly committed himself to teach the blind. This noble act occurred after he witnessed people being paraded around as court jesters or struggling on the streets as beggars. Mr. Hauly founded a residential school for blind children that featured teaching children how to read with raised print. Following the precedent set by Mr. Hauly, Mr. Samuel Gridley Howe founded the world-renowned Perkins School for the Blind in 1821 in the United States. A variety of curricula and methods were both piloted and refined at the Perkins School. Anne Sullivan and her well-known pupil, Helen Keller, spent several years at the Perkins School.

A little over a dozen years after the establishment of the Perkins School, a French man named Louis Braille created the Braille's system. The Braille system, as it is now referred to, is probably the most successful method for teaching touch-reading and has survived the test of time. It is simple, utilizing a six-dot cell system, but should never be perceived as simplistic.

In the second half of the nineteenth century, one of the major advances for the visually impaired was not targeted at blind or very low vision children but rather at children who appeared on the surface to have "normal" vision. In the 1860s, a Dutch ophthalmologist invented or developed the Snellen chart. This was an important creation since it was and currently still is the most widely used device for visual acuity screening of school age children.

The first major development for the severely visually impaired took place between 1900 and 1913. Classes in public schools were opened in Boston, Chicago, and Cleveland for children who were blind or had low vision. This was a significant development since several local school systems began to recognize that the government had an obligation to provide education for children with severe visual impairments. Following the establishment of the public school classes east of the Mississippi River, other school systems followed suit.

The next trend to provide blind individuals with government supported services occurred in 1932 when the U.S. Library of Congress made talking books available to all legally blind individuals. Also in the 1930s, a California school district employed itinerant teachers to help students with visual impairments function in regular education classrooms. During this time period, also in the U.S., there was the inauguration of orientation and mobility services including a white cane to help people function in the community.

In the second half of the 20th century, the Perkins braillewriter was invented at the Perkins School for the Blind. The braillewriter made it possible for individuals sitting at simple machines to transcribe books into a touch-reading format. This increased literacy among those with severe visual impairments. It is hoped that the advances for the visually impaired continue well into the 21st century.

Circle the letter of the best word or words to complete each sentence.

Example:
The best title for this article could possibly be:

    a. Key Developments Impacting those without Visual Impairments

    (b.) Key Developments Benefiting those with Visual Impairments

    c. The Visually Challenged in Your Community

    d. People Who Help the Visually Impaired

1. Individuals with low vision _____.

    a. can only see things that are low to the ground

    b. have very minimal sight and can only see things that are low to the ground

    c. have very minimal sight

    d. none of the above

2. **From the article, one can assume that Cleveland is _____.**

    a. within 100 miles of Boston

    b. within 100 miles of Chicago

    c. east of the Mississippi

    d. all of the above

3. **There have been certain residential schools founded for the blind. These include _____.**

    a. the school founded by Mr. Hauly

    b. the school founded by Mr. Perkins

    c. the schools founded by Mr. Gridley Howe and Mr. Perkins

    d. the schools founded Mr. Hauly and Mr. Gridley Howe

4. **All of the advances mentioned in this article took place in _____.**

    a. Europe

    b. the United States

    c. the United States and Europe

    d. none of the above

5. **The Braille system is _____.**

    a. simplistic

    b. simple

    c. simple and simplistic

    d. neither simple nor simplistic

6. **The Snellen chart is an important development _____.**

    a. because it helped children who were completely blind and had no vision

    b. because it only helped low vision children

    c. because it helped to identify children who both have visual impairments and attend regular public schools

    d. because an ophthalmologist was involved in the creation

7. **Although specific information was not given, one could assume that _____.**

    a. Dr. Snellen did not invent the Snellen chart

    b. Mr. Perkins developed the Snellen chart

    c. Dr. Snellen invented the Snellen chart

    d. Mr. Perkins and Mr. Braille developed the Snellen chart

8. **Talking books are only available for those _____.**

    a. who are legally blind

    b. who can not be legally blind

    c. who have hearing aids and are legally blind

    d. who have any visual impairments, even minor ones

9. **The white cane _____.**

    a. was designed to help the severely visually impaired students stay out of the community

    b. was designed to keep the blind in residential schools

    c. was inaugurated by the president of the Perkins school

    d. was designed to help individuals with visual impairments function in the community

10. **The Perkins braillewriter _____.**

    a. was the only invention in the 20th century that gave blind individuals access to books

    b. was invented by Mr. Perkins

    c. helped blind individuals have access to the printed word

    d. none of the above

Reading 4

The Critic's Corner

This week, I will be writing about a topic near and dear to my heart as well as the heart of my children. Don't underestimate the power or value of children's literature or "kiddie lit" as it is sometimes referred. Many individuals find it surprising that children's literature, even books with little text, frequently encompass social themes that span from environmental studies to psychology or sociology. For example, "The Giving Tree" by Shel Silverstein is a very simple but elegant black and white picture book that tells the story of a boy and a tree that are mutually dependent upon one another. As the story unfolds, the man exploits the tree, while the tree remains gracious and benevolent towards the man. This book makes a powerful statement concerning man's disregard and downright callousness towards the environment.

Judith Viorst, a satirist, has written a charming picture book entitled "Alexander and the Terrible, Horrible, No Good, Very Bad Day." Her work, illustrated with black and white drawings, deals with the frustrations confronting a very young boy. Through the voice of a child, she reveals the emotional issues impacting children including sibling rivalry, parental approval, and unrealistic teacher expectations. This book is invaluable for those wishing to study the psychological makeup of young children, mainly boys but also girls.

Another book with a minimal amount of print worth checking out is "A Chair for My Mother" by Vera Williams. The story of a family who has lost all of their belongings in a fire is told, in part, through brightly colored illustrations accompanied by text. The community pulls together to get the family back on their feet. In addition, the family helps itself reach a goal through hard work and stick-to-itiveness. This book addresses some key sociological support systems, including the extended family and the community.

So the next time you are in a bookstore or library, take a deep breath and a moment to stop and browse the children's book section.

Based on the article, circle the letter of the best answer to each question.

Example:
What is the main topic of this article?
(a.) Children's Literature
b. Remedies for Social Problems
c. Environmental Studies
d. none of the above

1. How does the writer of the article feel about children's literature?
a. The writer believes that it is a frivolous genre that should be dismissed.
b. The writer believes that it has a great deal of merit.
c. It isn't clear.
d. The writer feels that it should be rejected from people's hearts.

2. In the first paragraph the words *mutually dependent* are used. In this context, what does *mutually dependent* mean?
a. Both sides do NOT need one another.
b. One side needs the other.
c. Both sides need one another.
d. Everyone is dependent upon the environment.

3. Which book deals with issues impacting the environment?
a. "The Giving Tree"
b. "A Chair for My Mother"
c. both a and b
d. none of the above

4. Which books are illustrated with black and white drawings?
a. "The Giving Tree"
b. "Alexander and the Terrible, Horrible, No Good, Very Bad Day"
c. "A Chair for my Mother"
d. a and b

5. According to the article, what can one assume?
a. The writer has some familiarity with children's literature.
b. The writer has no familiarity with children's literature.
c. The writer doesn't want to read any more children's books.
d. The writer checks out a lot of books from the library.

6. **What did Judith Viorst, a mother herself, write?**

   a. a book using a mother's voice

   b. a book only suitable for mothers to read

   c. a book using the "voice" of a child

   d. a book that could never have been written by a satirist

7. **What was the psychological pressure, or pressures, mentioned in Judith Viorst's book?**

   a. sibling rivalry

   b. parental approval

   c. teacher satisfaction

   d. a and b but not c

8. **What happened to the family in Vera Williams's book?**

   a. They suffered from a fire.

   b. They survived the fire.

   c. a and b

   d. none of the above

9. **What does Vera Williams use to tell her story?**

   a. only text to write her story

   b. only text to relay her message

   c. only illustrations to relay her message

   c. text and illustrations to convey her message

10. **What is meant by the term *stick-to-itiveness*?**

    a. lazy

    b. someone involved in sticky situations

    c. someone who cannot work hard

    d. someone who keeps on working until a goal is achieved

Name _____   **Date** _____

1. **Match each word with its meaning. (5 points)**

   ___ 1. tuition   a. show

   ___ 2. relevance   b. surprised

   ___ 3. discipline   c. equal; alike

   ___ 4. status   d. fee (money) for school

   ___ 5. reflect   e. control

   ___ 6. afford   f. relating to the countryside

   ___ 7. determine   g. be the cause of something

   ___ 8. startled   h. have enough money for

   ___ 9. rural   i. social position or standing

   ___ 10. identical   j. importance

2. **Write *T* for true statements and *F* for false statements. (5 points)**

   ___ 1. Education is free for all students around the world.

   ___ 2. All secondary school have important national exams.

   ___ 3. The educational system is closely linked to the culture of the country.

   ___ 4. In the U.S., there are many part-time and older students in colleges.

   ___ 5. College life has changed a lot because of technology, especially the Internet.

3. **Circle the letter of the correct pronoun. (5 points)**

   1. Some students love ideas. _____ prefer the theory-to-practice method of learning

      a. They   b. Their   c. Them

   2. There are many part-time students. Time and money are important to _____.

      a. they   b. their   c. them

   3. American professors don't prefer the same learning style as _____ students.

      a. they   b. their   c. them

   4. Many students volunteer in the community. _____ hope to make changes in society.

      a. They   b. Their   c. Them

5. Most college professors have e-mail so students can talk with _____ about class work.

   a. they   b. their   c. them

4. Write the type of school. Use the choices from the box. (5 points)

college preparatory	vocational	primary
secondary	university	graduate

1. Students continue studies after elementary school in _____ schools.

2. Students continue studies in a specialized field after a bachelor's degree in _____ schools.

3. Students learn basic skills: reading, writing, grammar, mathematics, natural sciences, and social studies in _____ schools.

4. Students get job training in _____ schools.

5. Students study academic courses in preparation for university in _____ schools.

5. Write answers to the questions. Use complete sentences. (5 points)

1. What types of schools have you attended?

_____

_____

2. Is public education free or do students pay tuition in your country?

_____

_____

3. Who goes to secondary schools in your country?

_____

_____

4. Why do students in your country go to college? What do they usually study?

_____

_____

5. Is technology used in your school? How?

_____

_____

Name _____   **Date** _____

1. Match each word with its meaning. (5 points)

___	1. priorities	a.	center of attention or interest
___	2. predict	b.	really; in fact
___	3. focus	c.	find an answer to a problem
___	4. decrease	d.	rich; wealthy
___	5. commute	e.	become inferior in quality or condition
___	6. affluent	f.	tell about the future
___	7. efficiently	g.	become gradually less or smaller
___	8. actually	h.	a list of what is important
___	9. solve	i.	in an effective manner with little waste or expense
___	10. worsen	j.	travel to work and back

2. Write *T* for true statements and *F* for false statements. (5 points)

___ 1. Many cities have a problem with overcrowding.

___ 2. Other city problems are recycling, public parks, and too many trees.

___ 3. Traffic problems can be solved with creative solutions such as environmental laws.

___ 4. Indoor pollution can make people sick inside of buildings and schools.

___ 5. Some causes of sick-building syndrome are natural materials and good air ventilation systems.

3. Circle the letter of the correct part of speech of the underlined word. (5 points)

1. There was a large <u>crowd</u> of people outside the store.

   a. adjective   b. adverb   c. verb   d. noun

2. The mayor slowly <u>answered</u> the reporters' questions.

   a. adjective   b. adverb   c. verb   d. noun

3. The city's problems became <u>worse</u> as the population grew.

   a. adjective   b. adverb   c. verb   d. noun

4. The park was <u>beautifully</u> planned with plenty of trees and green space.

   a. adjective   b. adverb   c. verb   d. noun

5. The citizens found <u>answers</u> to the city's problems.

   a. adjective   b. adverb   c. verb   d. noun

4. **Write the category for the items. Use the choices from the box. (5 points)**

garbage	air pollution	environment
disease symptoms	transportation	city problems

1. crime, disease, traffic: _____

2. trash, bottles, old newspapers: _____

3. smoke, gases, radon, carbon monoxide: _____

4. headaches, infections, coughs: _____

5. trees, rivers, air: _____

5. **Write answers to the questions. Use complete sentences. (5 points)**

1. Describe your city or town.

   _____

   _____

2. What are some problems in your city or town?

   _____

   _____

3. What transportation systems do people use?

   _____

   _____

4. Is there a recycling problem? What materials are recycled?

   _____

   _____

5. Do you think cities will be better or worse in the future? Why?

   _____

   _____

Name _____   **Date** _____

1. Match each word with its meaning. (5 points)

___	1. poverty	a.	the ability to hold something
___	2. capacity	b.	without value or use
___	3. literacy	c.	from an unknown person or source
___	4. collateral	d.	the state of being poor
___	5. fund	e.	people who have their own small businesses
___	6. worthless	f.	the ability to read and write
___	7. peer pressure	g.	property promised as security for a loan
___	8. microentrepreneurs	h.	connected but secondary in importance
___	9. anonymous	i.	money that is available
___	10. subsidiary	j.	group members make sure others act appropriately

2. Write *T* for true statements and *F* for false statements. (5 points)

___ 1. Banks often lend money to people without property or collateral.

___ 2. In microlending, groups lend money to rich people to start small businesses.

___ 3. Many women have raised their social position after starting their own businesses.

___ 4. Microlending is always successful.

___ 5. People need money to be happy and to have healthy lives.

3. Circle the letter of the correct word. (5 points)

1. It's important to understand the _____ behind advertising.

   a. logic   b. logical   c. logically

2. Advertisers want _____ to buy their products.

   a. consume   b. consumers   c. consumable

3. Some advertisements are _____ in nature.

   a. violence   b. violently   c. violent

4. The advertising was _____ because many people bought the product.

   a. succeed   b. success   c. successful

5. I didn't like the commercial. It was very _____.

   a. offend   b. offense   c. offensive

4. Write the category for the items. Use the choices from the box. (5 points)

businesses	stock market	vehicles
marketing	social ills	lending conditions

1. character, business capability, property: _____

2. investor, company shares, risk: _____

3. hair salon, plant shop, restaurant: _____

4. violence, crime, no education: _____

5. advertising, products, consumers: _____

5. Write answers to the questions. Use complete sentences. (5 points)

1. Would you like to start your own business? Why or why not?

   _____

   _____

2. What are some reasons that people apply for loans?

   _____

   _____

3. How do you choose a product to buy?

   _____

   _____

4. Are there any good advertisements? Explain.

   _____

   _____

5. What types of advertisements do you think are effective?

   _____

   _____

Name _____   **Date** _____

1. Match each word with its meaning. (5 points)

___	1. livelihood	a.	certain; safe
___	2. stress	b.	disadvantage
___	3. self-confidence	c.	to draw attention away from something
___	4. challenge	d.	to improve
___	5. telecommuting	e.	a force that strains you emotionally
___	6. drawback	f.	able to change or adapt
___	7. upgrade	g.	a way of earning a living
___	8. distract	h.	something that tests your skills and resources
___	9. flexible	i.	belief in your own abilities
___	10. secure	j.	communicating through computer

2. Write *T* for true statements and *F* for false statements. (5 points)

___ 1. People around the world have more job security today than in the past.

___ 2. Some people become worried or depressed if they lose their jobs

___ 3. Technology has changed, but workers don't need to learn about the changes

___ 4. Classified ads and employment agencies are some ways to learn about technology.

___ 5. People can use the Internet to look for jobs.

3. Circle the letter of the correct word. (5 points)

1. John goes to school, but he also has a _____ -time job.

   a. self   b. computer   c. part

2. He is taking a _____ science course.

   a. traffic   b. shopping   c. computer

3. He plans to talk to the _____ counselor about future job possibilities.

   a. career   b. dream   c. mass

4. Do you plan to go to the _____ office to fill out a job application?

   a. personnel   b. city   c. classified

5. I grew up in a small town, but I love the _____ life.

   a. computer   b. job   c. city

4. Read the steps for finding a job. Number them in the correct order. (5 points)

____ Find a job board on the Internet.

____ Post your resume on the Internet.

____ Find a career that you love.

____ Get the skills and education you need for the career.

____ Go for a job interview.

5. Write answers to the questions. Use complete sentences. (5 points)

1. In your community, do workers have job security or do they change jobs often?

_____

_____

2. Where can people find out about job openings?

_____

_____

3. How is technology used in workplaces?

_____

_____

4. What is your dream job or profession?

_____

_____

5. What education or skills do you need for the job?

_____

_____

Name _____   **Date** _____

1. Match each word with its meaning. (5 points)

___	1. lifestyle	a.	money made in a business
___	2. slang	b.	put money into a business
___	3. fad	c.	a particular fashion
___	4. profit	d.	smell, fragrance
___	5. distinguish	e.	way of living; tastes and interests
___	6. invest	f.	how much something is worth
___	7. enroll	g.	something popular for a very short time
___	8. style	h.	recognize as being different
___	9. value	i.	enter or register; sign up for
___	10. aroma	j.	casual speech; popular language

2. Write *T* for true statements and *F* for false statements. (5 points)

___ 1. People follow fads because they want to be part of new things.

___ 2. A trend is a short fad.

___ 3. People in business don't pay attention to fads and trends.

___ 4. Tattoos are popular with older people.

___ 5. "Extreme sports" are for people who like excitement and danger.

3. Circle the letter of the correct suffix. (5 points)

1. We frequent_____ stop at the coffee shop after class.
   a. -ness   b. -ly   c. -ate

2. I can't concentr _____ with that loud music playing.
   a. -ate   b. -ation   c. -ism

3. We had an enjoy_____ time at the party.
   a. -able   b. -ly   c. -less

4. Don't forget to memor_____ your password.
   a. -ial   b. -ies   c. -ize

5. Their friend_____ means a lot to me.
   a. -ly   b. -less   c. -ship

4. Match the prefixes and roots to form words to complete the sentence. (5 points)

trans-	-national
mis-	-count
pre-	-late
inter-	-view
re-	-placed

1. This number cannot be correct. Let's _____ the supplies.

2. Before we read this article, let's _____ it.

3. I can't read Italian. Can you _____ this letter for me?

4. There were many different cultural groups represented at the _____ conference.

5. I can't find my book. I probably _____ it somewhere.

5. Write answers to the questions. Use complete sentences. (5 points)

1. What are some current fads in clothing or food?

_____

_____

2. Would you like to try an "extreme sport"? Why or why not?

_____

_____

3. Do you think life is too complicated? Why or why not?

_____

_____

4. What are some activities for a simple life?

_____

_____

5. Would you prefer to travel to work or to telecommute? Why?

_____

_____

Name _____   Date _____

1. Match each word with its meaning. (5 points)

___	1. benefit	a.	a break or opening
___	2. harbor	b.	surprising
___	3. gap	c.	to make less
___	4. subsidy	d.	something that blocks the way
___	5. standards	e.	water that moves periodically
___	6. obstacle	f.	financial assistance
___	7. reduce	g.	a safe sheltered port for ships
___	8. contribute	h.	to help in bringing about something
___	9. startling	i.	rules or models for judging quality
___	10. tide	j.	advantage

2. Write _T_ for true statements and _F_ for false statements. (5 points)

___ 1. Open trade is good for all countries.

___ 2. Governments cannot help economies much.

___ 3. Transportation is easier for a country with access to an ocean.

___ 4. Ecotourists like to visit art museums.

___ 5. It's always very expensive to travel.

3. Circle the correct participle to complete the sentence. (5 points)

1. We had a really **(excited / exciting)** vacation.

2. All the tourists were **(thrilled / thrilling)** when they saw the rare tropical bird.

3. We took a **(challenged / challenging)** climb up the side of a volcano.

4. At the end of the day, we were all very **(tired / tiring)**.

4. We spent a **(relaxed / relaxing)** day at the beach.

4. Circle the letter of the correct idiom or expression. (5 points)

1. Let's take a bus instead of a plane. I'd like to _____.

   a. get around   b. take my time   c. on my own

2. You might be able to _____ a good price on that plane ticket on the Internet.

   a. track down   b. hold back   c. in the market for

3. The trip was great. It was really _____.

   a. whodunit   b. rough it   c. out of this world

4. I don't want to travel with a large group. I'd rather go _____.

   a. on my own   b. private eye   c. get around

5. You can meet some interesting people _____.

   a. getting from one place   b. track down   c. on board

5. Write answers to the questions. Use complete sentences. (5 points)

1. Do you prefer to travel by car, bus, train, or plane? Why?

   _____

   _____

2. Where would you like to go on a trip?

   _____

   _____

3. Why do some people want to travel into space?

   _____

   _____

4. Why might tourists like to see your country?

   _____

   _____

5. Do you think ecotourism is good? Why or why not?

   _____

   _____

Name _____   **Date** _____

1. Match each word with its meaning. (5 points)

___	1. prey	a.	a group of similar animals
___	2. colony	b.	to get or learn by effort
___	3. degree	c.	rapid sounds that seem like speech
___	4. species	d.	animal that is hunted
___	5. gesture	e.	one of a series of steps; a relative amount
___	6. chatter	f.	make someone feel better
___	7. vocalize	g.	a group living together
___	8. acquire	h.	movement usually of arms, hands, or head
___	9. reassure	i.	standing on two feet
___	10. upright	j.	make sounds

2. Write *T* for true statements and *F* for false statements. (5 points)

___ 1. All animals have languages.

___ 2. Movements and body language are one way to communicate.

___ 3. Whales make sounds to communicate.

___ 4. Scientists believe that people speak differently to girl babies than to boy babies.

___ 5. Men and women have the same styles of talking.

3. Circle the letter of the correct word. (5 points)

1. We read a _____ version of the article.

   a. simply   b. simplify   c. simplified

2. The scientists will _____ their research results at the conference next week.

   a. present   b. presentation   c. presentable

3. Many _____ about the future have already come true.

   a. predicts   b. predictions   c. predictably

4. We will _____ stop at the animal research center to see Kanzi, the chimp.

   a. definite   b. definition   c. definitely

5. Did you ever try to have a _____ with an animal?

   a. converse   b. conversation   c. conversational

4. Write the category for each set of words. Use the categories in the box. (5 points)

symbols	body language	words for facts
scientists	vocalizations	words for theories

1. dance, grin, tail wagging: _____

2. lexigrams, hand signals: _____

3. believe, suggest, might: _____

4. evidence, known, proof: _____

5. clicks, words, songs, sounds: _____

5. Write answers to the questions. Use complete sentences. (5 points)

1. What are some ways that animals communicate?

_____

_____

2. Why do animals communicate with each other?

_____

_____

3. Who do you think talks more—men or women? Why?

_____

_____

4. What kinds of toys do you think boys and girls should play with? Why?

_____

_____

5. Do you think English is a good choice as an international language? Why or why not?

_____

_____

Name _____   **Date** _____

1. Match each word with its meaning. (5 points)

___ 1. target	a.	necessary; very important
___ 2. tunnel	b.	Islamic religious building
___ 3. mosque	c.	tell in advance; predict
___ 4. worship	d.	sacred; important for religious reasons
___ 5. foretell	e.	like; have a good opinion of
___ 6. depict	f.	desired goal
___ 7. admire	g.	very beautiful
___ 8. essential	h.	pray to; show great respect for
___ 9. exquisite	i.	building long underground passage
___ 10. holy	j.	describe or represent

2. Write *T* for true statements and *F* for false statements. (5 points)

___ 1. It may be possible to learn more about a culture in an art history class than in a history class.

___ 2. Cave art consists of mostly religious symbols.

___ 3. Some artists create pictures that give their opinions of political and social events.

___ 4. All art has practical and functional uses.

___ 5. Traditional art has had no influence in modern painters.

3. Look at the boldfaced words in the sentences. Circle + if the word has a positive connotation or - if it has a negative connotation. (5 points)

+ – 1. The emaciated horse walked slowly to the barn.

+ – 2. The ballet dancer was quite slender.

+ – 3. That dog can't run because it is so obese.

+ – 4. The little baby has chubby cheeks.

+ – 5. She had a plain face, but she was very friendly and likeable.

4. Write the relationship for these sets of words. Use the choices from the box. (5 points)

synonyms	noun to adjective	tool to use
antonyms	quantity of food	part to whole

1. city: urban _____

2. handsome: good-looking _____

3. dozen: eggs _____

4. brush: painting _____

5. ugly: beautiful _____

5. Write answers to the questions. Use complete sentences. (5 points)

1. Why do people create art?

_____

_____

2. What are some different forms of art?

_____

_____

3. In what ways do people try to make their bodies more beautiful?

_____

_____

4. What type of art is popular in your community?

_____

_____

5. What kinds of art do you prefer? Why?

_____

_____

Name _____   **Date** _____

1. Match each word with its meaning. (5 points)

___	1. origin	a.	the process of becoming full-grown
___	2. intuition	b.	ability to remember
___	3. maturation	c.	made visible or revealed
___	4. colleague	d.	a person who works in the same profession as another
___	5. exposed	e.	completely grown or developed
___	6. rotate	f.	understanding without reasoning or proof
___	7. repressed	g.	starting point, beginning
___	8. mature	h.	to turn around on a center
___	9. memory	i.	sleeplessness
___	10. insomnia	j.	held back; forced out of mind

2. Write *T* for true statements and *F* for false statements. (5 points)

___ 1. Creative people use the right side of the brain more than other people.

___ 2. Memories are always true.

___ 3. The brain is fully developed by the time a person is twelve years old.

___ 4. Personality is affected by both genes and the environment.

___ 5. Scientists can change the genes of people.

3. Circle the letter of the correct word. (5 points)

1. Margot didn't stop to think. She relied on her _____ to make her choice.

   a. logic   b. insight   c. knowledge

2. Jim had no problem thinking clearly about the present, but his _____ of his childhood years was very unclear.

   a. memory   b. mind   c. brain

3. I usually eat lunch with some of my _____ in the company cafeteria.

   a. peers   b. co-workers   c. bosses

4. We have a ladder, brushes, and rollers. Do we need any other _____ for painting the room?

    a. machine   b. device   c. equipment

5. The cerebrum and cerebellum are parts of the _____.

    a. brain   b. mind   c. memory

4. Write *F* for statements that are facts and *TH* for statements that are theories. (5 points)

    ___ 1. Scientists are certain that music can help children do better at math.

    ___ 2. It is possible that negative emotions can cause higher rates of sickness.

    ___ 3. They claim that we can be taught to use our right hemisphere more.

    ___ 4. It has been shown that our minds and bodies are closely connected.

    ___ 5. It is likely that women better understand emotional clues because they have a larger corpus callosum than men do.

5. Write answers to the questions. Use complete sentences. (5 points)

1. What is a special memory you have from your childhood?

_____

_____

2. Are you more creative or more logical? Do you use the right or left hemisphere of your brain more?

_____

_____

3. Should more art and music be taught in primary schools? Why or why not?

_____

_____

4. What are some behavioral characteristics that are inherited?

_____

_____

5. How can parents help their children?

_____

_____

Name _____   **Date** _____

1. Match each word with its meaning. (5 points)

___	1. breakthrough	a.	look at symptoms and identify a disease
___	2. diagnose	b.	become pregnant with a baby
___	3. treat	c.	quickly
___	4. conceive	d.	following standards of moral behavior
___	5. beneficial	e.	amount; available quantity
___	6. ethical	f.	take care of; try to cure
___	7. rapidly	g.	sudden and exciting discovery
___	8. concerns	h.	the state of being able to produce young
___	9. supply	i.	good; helpful
___	10. fertility	j.	worries; problems; questions

2. Write *T* for true statements and *F* for false statements. (5 points)

___   1. There have been few new discoveries in medical technology.

___   2. Ethical questions about medical technology are easy to answer.

___   3. People don't agree on the advantages of birth control pills and fertility drugs.

___   4. Some people are living longer due to better medical technology.

___   5. Medical tests and treatments are less expensive now.

3. Circle the letter of the correct word. (5 points)

1. The doctor will report his _____ when the test results are final.

    a. diagnose   b. diagnosis   c. diagnostic

2. Some _____ folk cures are very effective.

    a. tradition   b. traditional   c. traditionally

3. Some treatments have _____ lengthened the life expectancy of people.

    a. effect   b. effective   c. effectively

4. Many diseases are now _____ because of new technology and medicines.

    a. treat   b. treatment   c. treatable

5. People are beginning to _____ new medical practices and methods.

    a. accept   b. acceptance   c. acceptable

4. Write the category for each set of words. Use the choices from the box. (5 points)

emotions	symptoms of illnesses	beliefs
methods of diagnosis	physician's actions	folk cures

1. values, ethics, morals: _____

2. headache, fever, pain: _____

3. treatment, surgery: _____

4. anger, sadness, hatred: _____

5. tests, ultrasound, MRI: _____

5. Write answers to the questions. Use complete sentences. (5 points)

1. What types of medical technology have extended human life?

   _____

   _____

2. What are some problems associated with multiple births?

   _____

   _____

3. What types of folk cures do you feel are useful? For which problems?

   _____

   _____

4. When do you believe human life begins?

   _____

   _____

5. When do you believe a person is dead?

   _____

   _____

Name _____   **Date** _____

1. Match each word with its meaning. (5 points)

___	1. gossip	a.	titles of newspaper articles
___	2. editorials	b.	to investigate
___	3. tabloids	c.	rumors about personal affairs
___	4. headlines	d.	articles that give the opinions of the editors
___	5. register	e.	to connect; associate
___	6. customized	f.	newspapers that present sensational stories
___	7. scandal	g.	the act of chasing or trying to catch
___	8. pursuit	h.	shocking news about improper behavior
___	9. probe	i.	made to fit a person's interests and tastes
___	10. link	j.	to enroll or sign up for

2. Write *T* for true statements and *F* for false statements. (5 points)

___ 1. Reading an English-language newspaper doesn't help you learn English.

___ 2. Newspapers never have gossip or half-truths.

___ 3. Hard news should be subjective.

___ 4. Opinions and editorials are the same as hard news.

___ 5. Sports stories are usually very difficult to read.

3. Circle the letter of the correct meanings of the underlined words in the headlines. (5 points)

1. Police <u>Nab</u> Suspect

   a. have caught   b. are catching   c. will catch

2. Plane Crash <u>Kills</u> One

   a. is killing   b. has killed   c. may kill

3. President <u>Opts For</u> Tax Cut

   a. has prohibited   b. is decreasing   c. has chosen

4. Party Leader <u>Backing</u> New Mayor

   a. is supporting   b. has tried to escape from   c. is considering

5. Bank <u>Slashes</u> Fees

   a. has killed   b. has increased   c. has cut

4. Write the newspaper section for each of the articles. Use the choices from the box. (5 points)

"Hard News"	Advice Column	TV Programs and Reviews
Sports	Book Reviews	Editorials

1. Stars Outshoot Kings 5-4 _____

2. Hard Choices or Poor Planning? _____

3. State Budget Voted Down _____

4. *Poetry Alive* Tops Book List _____

5. New Show Smash Hit _____

5. Write answers to the questions. Use complete sentences. (5 points)

1. How often do you read an English-language newspaper?

   _____

   _____

2. What sections of newspapers do you prefer to read?

   _____

   _____

3. How do you choose which newspaper articles to read?

   _____

   _____

4. Have you ever used an online news service?

   _____

   _____

5. Is censorship of newspapers good or bad? Why?

   _____

   _____

Name _____   **Date** _____

1. Match each word with its meaning. (5 points)

___	1. rights	a.	penalty for a crime
___	2. duties	b.	to start legal proceedings against someone
___	3. punishment	c.	decision of a judge or court
___	4. deterrent	d.	disagreement or argument
___	5. sentence	e.	something a person should or must do
___	6. dispute	f.	to do
___	7. commit	g.	something that prevents an action
___	8. restore	h.	to break a law
___	9. sue	i.	something that a person has a moral or legal claim to
___	10. violate	j.	to put back to an original state

2. Write *T* for true statements and *F* for false statements. (5 points)

___ 1. Not all societies have laws.

___ 2. The idea of "right" and "wrong" are not the same in all cultures.

___ 3. The punishment for stealing is always returning the stolen items.

___ 4. A jury is always used to settle disputes.

___ 5. In some societies, traditional justice is used along with modern court systems.

3. Circle the letter of the correct word. (5 points)

1. An action may be _____ a crime in one country but not in another.
   a. consider   b. considered   c. considering

2. There is a difference between _____ religious laws and laws of the government.
   a. break   b. broken   c. breaking

3. Punishment may _____ people from committing more crimes.
   a. prevent   b. prevented   c. preventing

4. Miriam Wilgnal wanted to _____ high school.
   a. finish   b. finished   c. finishing

5. The judge _____ in her favor.
   a. rule   b. ruled   c. ruling

4. Write the category for each set of words. Use the choices from the box. (5 points)

education	journalism	business
medical	religion	legal

1. dispute, deterrent, sue: _____

2. lecture, assignment, graduate: _____

3. treatment, disease, cure: _____

4. faith, worship, sin: _____

5. credit, budget, marketing: _____

5. Write answers to the questions. Use complete sentences. (5 points)

1. Why are laws important?

   _____

   _____

2. Which is more important to you—rights of the individual or social harmony? Why?

   _____

   _____

3. What types of punishment do you think are not effective?

   _____

   _____

4. Which do you feel is more important—traditional or modern justice?

   _____

   _____

5. How do you feel about the system of laws and justice in the United States?

   _____

   _____

Placement Test Answer Key

Part 1 Determining Meaning and Usage from Context

Example: d

1. b
2. d
3. a
4. c
5. d
6. a
7. d
8. a
9. a
10. c

Part 2 Idiomatic Expressions

Example: a

1. c
2. b
3. d
4. c
5. c

Part 3 Scanning for Members of Word Families

Example: b

1. a
2. b
3. d
4. c
5. b

Part 4 Reading Comprehension

Reading 1

Example: F

1. F
2. T
3. F
4. F
5. F

Reading 2

Example: F

1. F
2. T
3. F
4. T
5. F

Reading 3

Example: b

1. c
2. c
3. d
4. c
5. b
6. c
7. c
8. a
9. d
10. c

Reading 4

Example: a

1. b
2. c
3. a
4. d
5. a
6. c
7. d
8. c
9. c
10. d

Answer Keys for Chapter Quizzes

Chapter 1

1.
1. d
2. j
3. e
4. i
5. a
6. h
7. g
8. b
9. f
10. c

2.
1. F
2. F
3. T
4. T
5. T

3.
1. a
2. c
3. b
4. a
5. c

4.
1. secondary
2. graduate
3. primary
4. vocational
5. college preparatory

5. Answers will vary.

Chapter 2

1.
1. h
2. f
3. a
4. g
5. j
6. d
7. i
8. b
9. c
10. e

2.
1. T
2. F
3. F
4. T
5. F

3.
1. d
2. c
3. a
4. b
5. d

4.
1. city problems
2. garbage
3. air pollution
4. disease symptoms
5. environment

5. Answers will vary.

Chapter 3

1.
1. d
2. a
3. f
4. g
5. i
6. b
7. j
8. e
9. c
10. h

2.
1. F
2. F
3. T
4. F
5. F

3.
1. a
2. b
3. c
4. c
5. c

4.
1. lending conditions
2. stock market
3. businesses
4. social ills
5. marketing

5. Answers will vary.

Chapter 4

1.
1. g
2. e
3. i
4. h
5. j
6. b
7. d
8. c
9. f
10. a

2.
1. F
2. T
3. F
4. F
5. T

3.
1. c
2. c
3. a
4. a
5. c

4. 3, 4, 1, 2, 5

5. Answers will vary.

Chapter 5

1.
1. e
2. j
3. g
4. a
5. h
6. b
7. i
8. c
9. f
10. d

2.
1. T
2. F
3. F
4. F
5. T

3.
1. b
2. a
3. a
4. c
5. c

4.
1. recount
2. preview
3. translate
4. international
5. misplaced

5. Answers will vary.

Chapter 6

1.
1. j
2. g
3. a
4. f
5. i
6. d
7. c
8. h
9. b
10. e

2.
1. T
2. F
3. T
4. F
5. F

3.
1. exciting
2. thrilled
3. challenging
4. tired
5. relaxing

4.
1. b
2. a
3. c
4. a
5. c

5. Answers will vary.

Chapter 7

1.
1. d
2. g
3. e
4. a
5. h
6. c
7. j
8. b
9. f
10. i

2.
1. F
2. T
3. T
4. T
5. F

3.
1. c
2. a
3. b
4. c
5. b

4.
1. body language
2. symbols
3. words for theories
4. words for facts
5. vocalizations

5. Answers will vary.

Chapter 8

1.
1. f
2. i
3. b
4. h
5. c
6. j
7. e
8. a
9. g
10. d

2.
1. T
2. F
3. F
4. T
5. F

3.
1. –
2. +
3. –
4. +
5. +

4.
1. noun to adjective
2. synonyms
3. quantity of food
4. tool to use
5. antonyms

5. Answers will vary.

Chapter 9

1.
1. g
2. f
3. a
4. d
5. c
6. h
7. j
8. e
9. b
10. i

2.
1. T
2. F
3. F
4. T
5. F

3.
1. b
2. a
3. b
4. c
5. a

4.
1. F
2. TH
3. TH
4. F
5. TH

5. Answers will vary.

Chapter 10

1.
1. g
2. a
3. f
4. b
5. i
6. d
7. c
8. j
9. e
10. h

2.
1. F
2. F
3. T
4. T
5. F

3.
1. b
2. b
3. c
4. c
5. a

4.
1. beliefs
2. symptoms of illnesses
3. physicians' actions
4. emotions
5. methods of diagnosis

5. Answers will vary.

Chapter 11

1.
1. c
2. d
3. f
4. a
5. j
6. i
7. h
8. g
9. b
10. e

2.
1. F
2. F
3. F
4. F
5. T

3.
1. a
2. b
3. c
4. a
5. c

4.
1. Sports
2. Editorials
3. "Hard News"
4. Book Reviews
5. TV Programs and Reviews

5. Answers will vary.

Chapter 12

1.
1. i
2. e
3. a
4. g
5. c
6. d
7. f
8. j
9. b
10. h

2.
1. F
2. T
3. F
4. F
5. T

3.
1. b
2. c
3. a
4. a
5. b

4.
1. legal
2. education
3. medical
4. religion
5. business

5. Answers will vary.